Mountain Charley
or the
Adventures of Mrs. E. J. Guerin,
Who Was Thirteen Years in Male Attire

MOUNTAIN CHARLEY

or the
Adventures of Mrs. E. J. Guerin,
Who Was Thirteen Years in Male Attire

An Autobiography Comprising a Period of Thirteen Years Life
in the States, California, and Pike's Peak

With an Introduction by
FRED M. MAZZULLA AND WILLIAM KOSTKA

UNIVERSITY OF OKLAHOMA PRESS
NORMAN

921
Guie

Lewiston City Library
Lewiston, Idaho 83501

Library of Congress Catalog Card Number: 68-15671

New edition copyright © 1968 by the University of Oklahoma Press, Norman, Publishing Division of the University. Manufactured in the U.S.A. First printing of the new edition, 1968; second printing, 1985.

1823.9058
87-2525

INTRODUCTION

By Fred M. Mazzulla and William Kostka

THIS AUTOBIOGRAPHY of Mountain Charley is the story of an intriguing character of the West and the Colorado Gold Rush era. The story is especially fascinating because Mountain Charley was a woman, one of the earliest of the captivating young ladies whose exploits add spice to the chronicles of the times.

In the beginning, her story reads like a romanticized novel; further on, however, her tale rings with more than a semblance of truth. This is particularly illustrated by the description of Mountain Charley's wagon trek to California in the spring of 1855. She kept a diary on this trip, with detailed records of such trail markers as Court House and Chimney Rock, Scott's Bluff, Mormon Ferry, and Independence Rock, which guided the California and Oregon wagon trains.

There is an even greater ring of authenticity after Mountain Charley, lured by a new bonanza, appeared along with the first of the Pikes Peak gold seekers in the spring of 1859. The places mentioned, misspelled as they often were in those days, still exist. There is a record of the Denver saloon she claims to have owned twice during her short stay in the mining regions. It was called the Mountain Boy's Saloon. A saloon of that name is described in the 1866 Denver Directory as the fourth building on the right, walking eastward from Cherry Creek along Blake Street. This was one of Denver's principal business streets in 1860, when Mountain Charley owned the saloon and married her bartender, H. L. Guerin. In the fall of 1860, she left with Guerin to return to the East.

The Russell brothers, as well as John H. Gregory, have been credited with first or prior discovery of Pikes Peak gold. Researchers will strike high-grade ore in the last chapter where Mountain Charley records verbatim, two authentic, non-conflicting statements. By the way, who *was* first?

Mrs. E. J. Guerin published her autobiography of Mountain Charley in Dubuque, Iowa, in 1861. It was "published for the author," and the book's subhead reads: "An Autobiography Comprising a Period of Thirteen Years Life in the States, California, and Pike's Peak." The author probably had only a few copies printed, and they soon disappeared. By 1953, when Charles L. Camp revised the third edition of Henry R. Wagner's *The Plains and the Rockies* (a bibliography of original narratives of travel and adventure from 1860 to 1865), only one copy was known to exist. That copy was in the private collection of Fred Rosenstock and later sold by him to Everett L. DeGolyer, Jr., of Dallas, Texas, its present owner, who generously allowed it to be used for this edition.

This Western Frontier Library edition of the autobiography of Mountain Charley is, of course, not a facsimile of the original; however, the text remains unchanged. None of its flaws, such as the omission of Chapter VIII, are corrected. Apparently, either the author or the printer inadvertently skipped Chapter VIII as the original narrative flows smoothly from Chapter VII directly into Chapter IX.

In the daily diary after the date July 31 is reached, some puzzling dates follow with no month named until another

"31st of July" is reached. That was the day Mountain Charley climbed a mountain and saw Salt Lake seventy-five miles away to the west. In August, Mountain Charley, the men of the train, and their mules and cattle are described as plodding ankle-deep in soda and alkali dust across the desert beyond Salt Lake.

Is it possible that Mrs. Guerin decided to publish her autobiography so quickly after returning to "the States" because she had heard of other young ladies who also claimed to be Mountain Charley? Anyone who has researched the early public press of the West has encountered other stories about Mountain Charley. He will be perplexed if he tries to reconcile the facts in each tale with Mrs. Guerin's autobiography, with the purpose of compiling the one authentic account of Mountain Charley's adventures.

At least three of these tales are well known, and further research might reveal others. The first story was published on September 10, 1859, in Denver's *Rocky Mountain News;* a second in the Leadville, Colorado, *Daily Chronicle* on July 15, 1879; and the third and longest in the *Colorado Transcript* of Golden, Colorado, in January, February, and March, 1885.

The *Rocky Mountain News* story bears some points of similarity to the autobiography of Mrs. E. J. Guerin. It is based on a story in an eastern newspaper written by a correspondent, possibly Horace Greeley himself, who is supposed to have mentioned Mountain Charley in his letters from the western gold fields to the New York *Tribune*. The story gives Mountain Charley's maiden name as Elsa Jane Forest, which is compatible with "Mrs. E. J. Guerin." Other facts, such as the Louisiana background, widowhood at sixteen, residence in St. Louis before donning masculine garb, and driving mules and cattle to California, are similar to those in the autobiography. In September, 1859, she already had been at the Colorado diggings for a month. The *News*, in repeating the eastern journal's story, referred to it as "admirable fiction," written with "emotions of pity" and wished that the "eastern journal could but once see the veritable and notorious 'Charley' as she is familiarly called in the mines, smoking, drinking, swearing and taking equal part in the amusements of a crowd of loafers—it would open their eyes."

Twenty years after the *Rocky Mountain News* story and eighteen years after the publication of Mrs. Guerin's autobiography, a story headlined "Mountain Charley" appeared in the Leadville *Daily Chronicle* of July 15, 1879. The final sentence reads: "The only purpose the reporter had in penning this essay was to tell that Mountain Charley is now an inmate of Leadville." The yarn relates her work as a clerk in a Central City, Colorado Territory, store while known as "Charley Walworth," her enlistment under the name of Jackson Snow in the Fifth Wisconsin Infantry, and, in 1866, her employment as a gambling-house operator and real-estate speculator in Cheyenne, Wyoming Territory, "where her career became generally known, and the papers gave her the name of Mountain Charley."

In January, 1885, General George West, publisher of the *Colorado Transcript*, in Golden, Colorado, issued his version of the "Mountain Charley" he knew. (See *Colorado Transcript*, January 14, 1885, February 25, 1885, March 4, 1885, March 11, 1885.) He had kept his promise not to publish her story for twenty-five years after she had revealed her background to him in December, 1859. This Charley, who said her proper name was Charlotte, came from Iowa, where her mother had died when Charlotte was eighteen. The following year, she ran off with a "dandified looking young man" whom she married in Des Moines. After her baby was born dead, he deserted her for another woman. Mountain Charley assumed that her errant gambler husband had gone to Pikes Peak. In the summer of 1859, she dressed in men's clothing and sought him and his "low-down wench" to take her revenge. According to West, she "found them."

Late in the fall of 1860, West received a letter from her from Albuquerque, New Mexico, and in 1861, the year this autobiography was published, West saw her in Denver. Dressed as an attractive blonde, she was dealing faro in Dick Wootton's Saloon "on Ferry Street." George West saw her for the last time in 1864 during the Civil War campaign in Missouri. Mountain Charley, an enlisted man, was then serving as an orderly for Union General Samuel R. Curtis.

George West's article was read by Mountain Charley in Iowa, and she immediately wrote him, sending her diary of service in the Civil War. She had enlisted in the Iowa Cavalry under the name of Charles Hatfield. Among the Second Colorado Cavalry and First Colorado Battery, serving with West in Missouri, she had recognized several Colorado men. While acting as a spy in woman's clothing in a Confederate camp, she had recognized some early Colorado miners, including Colonel George A. Jackson of the First Battalion of Arizona Sharpshooters. Jackson was one of the first men to discover gold in the Colorado mountains.

Mountain Charley, or Charles Hatfield, later was wounded and her true sex discovered by two doctors, who kept her secret. She was promoted to the rank of first lieutenant before being mustered out at Des Moines, Iowa, at the end of the war.

In 1885, when Mountain Charley wrote West, she had four children and had been married for eighteen years to a man she was sure West had known during the Colorado gold rush. The Golden *Transcript* reported that the West story of "Mountain Charley" was republished later in the *Rocky*

Mountain Herald, and also in a G.A.R. publication in Ohio. West's interesting account of the Mountain Charley he knew is appended to Mrs. Guerin's autobiography.

Whether Mountain Charley was one unique young woman or several interesting young ladies masquerading in men's clothing cannot be determined. Like Isabella Bird, the English gentlewoman in bloomers who climbed Longs Peak and rode alone through the Colorado wilderness, one or all of the Mountain Charleys were seeking freedom from the repressions of the Victorian Age.

PREFACE

THE AUTOBIOGRAPHY given in the following pages is literal actual fact, except so far as the conversations and incidents of one or two dramatic scenes are concerned. Hundreds of people who knew Mrs. Adams in Pike's Peak, (where the secret of her sex was first discovered) can bear witness to the truthfulness of what would otherwise seem an exaggerated fiction.

CONTENTS

Introduction, by Fred M. Mazzulla and
   William Kostka *page vii*

Author's Preface *xiii*

Mountain Charley or the Adventures of Mrs. E. J. Guerin,
   Who Was Thirteen Years in Male Attire 3

Mountain Charley: Colorado Story of Love, Lunacy and
   Revenge (from the *Colorado Transcript,* of Golden) 63

Mountain Charley

or the

Adventures of Mrs. E. J. Guerin,
Who Was Thirteen Years in Male Attire

MOUNTAIN CHARLEY

AN AUTOBIOGRAPHY

CHAPTER I

IN ABOUT THE YEAR 1830, there lived near Baton Rouge a planter in comfortable circumstances. His ancestry were of French origin and he, himself, although thoroughly Americanized, possessed a mixture in his character of French blood, which harmonized well with, while it tamed down the peculiarities which distinguished those who are born and bred under the influences of our free institutions.

This gentleman as I have said was a planter in comfortable circumstances—better than this, he was young, honorable, influential. His name I dare not give for reasons which will shortly appear, and it will answer my purpose and satisfy the legitimate curiosity of my readers if I call him Vereau.

With this hasty introduction of a gentleman, I pass to introduce one of an opposite sex.

She of whom I speak was at that time aged about twenty years, and was the daughter of a clergyman living in the glorious Empire State. Of her looks, it matters little—she was neither beautiful, nor was she the opposite. A plain countenance marked more by an expression of sweetness than brilliancy—an intelligent countenance—and one that possessed as its most remarkable feature, the peculiarity of becoming handsome only as the soul within was developed—was her possession. A well developed healthy form, of medium proportions, a well cultivated understanding and one possessing more than an average share of originality and force were the main points characterizing this lady of whom I am writing.

She too, must I, as in the case of the gentleman whose likeness preceded hers, introduce under a borrowed name, and for the same reason. Let me simply call her Anna Baldwin.

Having introduced my two characters separately, let me present them together. Why not? He, young, wealthy, honorable; she also young, also intelligent—why not bring them together? There is an eternal fitness in all things, and nothing more so than in the case of man and woman.

This being admitted, I will act in accordance with its conclusions.

It is a beautiful evening in September, and a magnificent steamer is parting swiftly the turbid waters of the Mississippi, with her prow turned towards the Gulf. At the time of which I speak, the boat is not far above New Orleans. Seated upon the hurricane deck, are a gentlemen and lady. They are near enough together to indicate a more than ordinary familiarity, a conclusion more fully shown in the circumstance that the gentleman in converse, bows his head close to that of the lady, and his words are lower than those in which people speak whose subject is an indifferent one. She listens too with a deeper interest seemingly, than would one whose ears were simply filled with commonplaces about the weather, the moonlight, or the peculiarities of the passing scenery.

"When I return from Kentucky," said he, "then shall I claim you as my wife. I would that ere I leave you we could be united, and thus place beyond the remotest doubt any danger of an exposure. But this cannot be for reasons I have shown you."

"But, oh! Henry, suppose something *should* happen—that

you should be killed or should be overtaken by one of the thousand accidents that waylay the traveler, and thus prevent you making the only reparation in human reach; suppose——"

"Oh, you are too fearful, Anna. You allow yourself to be afflicted by the faintest of suppositions. There is not the slightest chance of my being absent more than two months at farthest, and then——"

"God grant it! for should you fail me, there is but one remedy for my coming shame, and that, though terrible, would then be desirable."

"Do not doubt anything dearest, you have no reason to doubt my faith, for God knows I love only you, and to save you a single pang I would esteem no sacrifice too great. And in this case have I not every reason to fulfil my pledges? Are we not now man and wife by the solemnest ties that can bind man to woman? To be sure we lack that outward ceremonial which custom and society demand, yet lacking this, I would esteem myself a thousand times a villain did I do aught than fulfil to the letter, the holy relations which we in all truth and honesty now sustain, as much as if the priest had cemented our union with his blessing."

"I believe you my own husband, yet like a timid woman I tremble at a shadow—a something of which I know nothing."

"I cannot, nor do I blame you, yet be assured that I shall do only that which shall prove your fears to be groundless."

From this conversation the reader will obtain some insight into the character of the relations existing between the two individuals. I need add but a few words to fully explain it all.

A few months before, Anna Baldwin had left her home in New York to visit some relations at the South, among whom was a sister living at Baton Rouge. While there, she made the acquaintance of Vereau, and the acquaintance soon ripened into a warm attachment, as honorable on his side as it was devoted on hers.

And yet at one unlucky moment in their intercourse, Passion had usurped the domain of affection.

Circumstances which I need not particularize, as it is not necessary to the development of the subsequent history which I am about to relate, prevented him at once making the reparation which he desired, and the only one that the world will accept; and thus the matter had passed along until the time at which they are found on the passage to New Orleans.

He had shortly before received a letter from Kentucky informing him that he had become a co-heir in some property left by a deceased relative. The matter required his immediate attendance, and it was arranged that during his absence, she should visit New Orleans. He was to visit Frankfort, attend to his business, and upon his return they were to be united.

Leaving her at New Orleans, he set out for Kentucky. In a week or so after his departure, Miss Baldwin received a letter from her sister at Baton Rouge informing her that she was dangerously ill, and imploring her to return immediately. She did so, but upon her arrival found her sister convalescing rapidly.

I mention this circumstance for the reason that it had an important bearing upon Miss Baldwin's entire future. Hitherto twice or thrice each week the mail had brought her letters from Vereau, in which she was informed of the progress of his journey, his safe arrival at Frankfort and the rapid approach to completion of his business affairs, and all filled with protestations of earnest love and anticipations of a happy future. She had been in Baton Rouge but a little over two weeks, when suddenly his letters ceased. She awaited in anxious suspense a whole week—no letter. Another week dragged heavily, and her anxiety became a terrible fear. Was he sick and unable to write—was he dead—or, still more terrible thought, had he proven false? This last suggestion came like a mocking devil, and was at first repulsed, but again and again it made its appearance as time wore away. If sick, he would have directed some one else to write and inform her or his friends of the fact; if dead, the circumstance would have become known in a community in which he was so well known. There was but one conclusion at last, and that was that he had proved a traitor to his oaths and his manhood.

I will not dwell upon the agony, the despair, the fearful tortures that assailed the soul of Anna Baldwin as this fearful surmise finally grew into a fixed conclusion. The pages of fiction have a thousand times embodied such sad facts, and skilful writers have a thousand times dissected such minds and laid their secrets open to the inspection of the world. I will only say that in frenzy of agony, rage and shame that accompanied the sad conviction that she was ruined and betrayed, she listened to the addresses of an overseer on a neighboring plantation, and within a month from the time Vereau's correspondence ceased, she married him. The overseer was a drunken, worthless vagabond, who was only too glad to obtain so respectable a prize, even though encumbered as it was—a point on which he had been informed, but which he very willingly overlooked in consideration of getting a wife from a sphere so much above the one in which he moved.

There was the usual amount of wonderment at so unequal a match and much mortification among many of the gentlemen who had been indirectly suitors for Miss Baldwin's hand. There was the usual amount of tea-table talk and scandal among the ladies of her acquaintance, but heedless of it all, but she buried herself and her sad secret in the indifferently comfortable home which she was carried by her husband.

Just one week from the day that she was united in marriage with the overseer, she was wandering listlessly a short distance from her home. Buried in her sad thoughts, she did not perceive a traveling carriage which was coming toward her, and proceeding rapidly in the direction of the city. It came opposite to her, drove a little past and halted, a gentleman descended from the vehicle, and the next instant she was clasped in the arms of—Vereau!

"Henry!"

"Anna!"

The next instant she laid lifeless in his arms. Carrying her to a stream close by, he sprinkled her face with water, and soon she opened her eyes.

"Dear Henry," she murmured as she hid her face close upon his bosom. "Oh! are you alive? I have had such a terrible dream. I thought you were dead, and I thought myself married!"

"Oh, nonsense darling, here I am all right, and only surprised to find you away out here."

"Is it really you Henry?" said she, raising her head and passing her hand across her brow with a bewildered air. "I really thought or dreamed that you had left me forever, and that I had married a man whom I despised. Where are we—how came we here—did we ride out from the city?" said she as her eye fell upon the carriage.

"No, darling. You know I left Frankfort to go to Virginia, and was detained there some weeks longer than I expected. I returned by way of C—— and took a private carriage from there to the city. Right here, I found you, and——you know the rest."

Growing consciousness was returning to her soul as she listened to and in part comprehended what he was saying. But Miss Baldwin possessed a mind of more than common force. She did not faint as the iron entered her soul—as the conviction come upon her that there was a fearful mystery somewhere—but above all, that she was utterly lost. She did not even quiver as the conclusion came upon her like a white hot dagger being driven slowly into her warm heart. Only her countenance grew paler and her heart seemed about to burst, so fierce were its throbbings as she asked in a very low tone:

"Did you write me that you were going to leave Frankfort?"

"I did, didn't you get the letter? But—good God! what makes you look so pale!"

"Nothing—I'll tell you all in a moment—let me sit here." And she withdrew herself entirely from his arms, where she had lain, and staggered to a little mound a few feet off.

Then, with the only sign of life about her being the movement of her colorless lips and a convulsive twitching of her fingers, she told him all. Told him how all at once his letters had ceased—how day by day surprise had grown into anxiety, anxiety into suspense, this into despair, and finally, despair into desperation. And at last she was nearing the conclusion. She hesitated—the words would *not* come, but she forced them out—

"I—I—am—married!"

He sprang to his feet as if thrown there by an electric shock, and stood for an instant as if turned to stone, gazing at her who sat looking so mournfully at him.

"Treachery, by G—d!" at length burst from his lips, and turning upon his heel he strode toward the carriage. A deep groan from Anna caused him involuntarily to look around.

She had fallen lifeless to the ground—her rigid, marble countenance turned upward. He returned, bent over her and impressed one passionate kiss upon her lips, and then walked to the carriage, entered and was driven away.

Some two or three hours after Anna was aroused by a rough voice—

"What in h—ll are you layin' out here for? Get up and get some supper, can ye, or will ye lay there all night?"

Anna arose, and without replying went back to the cabin. The next day a city paper contained the following:

> PERSONAL—We regret to announce that our fellow citizen, HENRY VEREAU, Esq., left last evening with the intention of visiting France. He returned yesterday from a prolonged absence East, and found here upon his arrival, intelligence which determined him to leave immediately. The length of his absence is not certain. While all will join us in regrets at his departure, they will none the less unite with us in wishing him a prosperous voyage, happy visit and a speedy return.

I will close this chapter by adding one more item of a "personal" character, and that is, that I am the daughter of Henry Vereau and her who was once named Anna Baldwin.

CHAPTER II

THE CIRCUMSTANCES I have related in the foregoing chapter, I became acquainted with many years after the occurrence, and at a time when I too had begun to play a comparatively important part on life's stage. So also did I learn of the events of the four or five years which followed—a portion of which I shall now proceed to relate.

My first recollections are of a handsome residence situated in the country, of negroes—and one in particular, an old negress whom I called Mama—and of a tall, dark, melancholy gentleman whom I always termed Uncle. My remembrances of the place and its people are misty—all about it seem more like something I once saw in a dream, but whose characters time has effaced.

My uncle, as I can remember, was retiring in his disposition, scarcely ever visiting any one and not more frequently receiving any visitors. He was always taciturn, yet, when he did speak to me, it was always kindly and sometimes even tenderly. I can remember that I loved him very dearly, yet always stood somewhat in awe of him—he seemed so distant from anything that I could love or understand.

I also remember that sometimes an odd-looking wagon drawn by an old bony, melancholy horse, used to, at long intervals, drive up the long lane that led to the house from the main road. Then an old negro would assist out a pale sickly woman, who, invariably, would clasp me in her arms and covering me with kisses, call me her "dear child." She always brought me some little trifle—a bright piece of calico for a new apron for my doll, or some such childish gift. As long as she would stay, she would hold me in her lap and talk to me very kindly. On such occasions I was often surprised to find her eyes filled with tears, while her voice would be choked with sobs. When she came she never seemed to have any business except to see and talk with me, for I never knew her to ask any one else any questions unless I was absent.

During her visits, my uncle seemed always to be absent, for only upon one or two occasions did he ever make his appearance, and then he scarcely spoke, but hurried through the room into his office.

Sometimes I would get into the rough old wagon and drive away with this pale, strange woman, whom, at her request, I always called Aunt Anna. After a long drive, we would stop at a poor little cabin a good ways from a beautiful house on a hill, and there I have sometimes stayed for two or three days. There was a rough man there who always spoke in a savage manner to Aunt Anna; he had red, fierce eyes, and he used terrible oaths sometimes, and a great many times a day he would go to an old wooden chest in the corner and drink something out of an old dirty jug with a string tied around it for a handle. Aunt Anna never seemed to speak to him, never replied when he cursed her as he used to sometimes, and in short, seemed to pay no more attention to him than if he had been a post. Sometimes when I would return into the cabin after he had left, I would find her crying, but she would always say, when I asked her what was the matter, that she was sick—her heart pained her, she said.

And thus passed the time until I was five years of age, and then I was sent away down the river to great city—as it seemed then—New Orleans, where I was put to school.

These recollections of my earlier life which I have just attempted to give, are scarcely distinct enough in my memory to be recorded as facts. Yet sometimes in looking back, I see, as if surrounded by a mist, the scenes which I have attempted to describe, and a thousand others which I have not space to speak of, or which merge from the stronger outlines into indistinctness, so that I shall not attempt to speak of them. The last thing in this portion of my life that I remember from its vividness, was, that the day before I left for school, Aunt Anna came to see me, and cried over me at parting as if her heart were breaking. She gave me a small gold piece attached to a ribbon (I have it yet) as she left me, and made me promise between her sobs, not to forget Aunt Anna. I never saw her again—but, while at school, I received every month a letter full of earnest love, which, for awhile, was read to me by my teacher; but I soon became able to read them for myself. I remember one peculiarity in the letters, and that was, that when I was ten or twelve years of age, her letters were precisely the same character that they were in the beginning. That is, she always seemed to write as if I were still a little girl with the same thoughts and capacity that I was at the time I left her, or as if she always regarded me as being the same as when I left her.

My uncle wrote me at longer intervals in a letter which was enclosed in one to the principal, Madame T——. They always contained some good advice and were generally kind, but sometimes merely formal. He always enclosed me some money for my own private use, but the expenses of my tuition and clothing were given to the Principal. About once in each year, generally in the winter, he would come to New Orleans to spend a few weeks, and then he always called to see me, took me out riding and to places of amusement, and seemed much interested in my progress in study.

My life passed without much variation till I reached the age of twelve years, at which time an event occurred that had a marked bearing on my whole life, and gave it a direction never before traveled by any other woman. I had developed with a rapidity marvelous even in that hotbed, the South, and upon reaching the age of twelve, I was as much a woman in form, stature and appearance as most women at sixteen. My mind was, perhaps, not so much in advance of my years, yet, it was not of a character to do discredit to my appearance of maturity.

Without dwelling upon my peculiarities of character to an extent that would justify people in calling me egotistical, I would say that from the fact of my being so long thrown among strangers and all along accustomed to depend upon myself, I had attained a strength of character, a firmness, and self-reliance, that amounted to almost masculine force. In addition to this I was impetuous, self-willed—traits induced by the peculiarities of my surroundings, and whose existence will account for much of the strangeness of my subsequent career.

The important event to which I have made reference, is my marriage. I became acquainted with a gentleman whose appearance pleased me. He sought an introduction, obtained it, and as he could not visit the school, our communications were necessarily clandestine. I will not stop at the details of this portion of my life—suffice it to say, that it did [not] take long for him to win the heart of an inexperienced girl, and after that point was gained the next step was an easy one. He did not persuade me long ere I consented, and one morning the boarders at Madame T——'s numbered one less. I had packed up everything I could conveniently carry, made my exit through a window, and soon after was standing before a clergyman and was united for better or worse, to him to whom I had given the first fruits of my affections.

I subsequently ascertained that my husband was a pilot on the Mississippi—a fact of which I had never thought to inquire prior to our marriage. He was a noble fellow, and well repaid the sacrifice I had made for him. We made a pleasant trip to various cities in the South, and at the end of a month or so, came to St. Louis and determined to settle there permanently. My husband rented a small, comfortable house, and I was installed as its mistress.

Life flowed on in quiet, uninterrupted beauty. I wrote to my uncle, and also to Aunt Anna, informing them of the step I had taken, assuring them that I did not regret it, and that I was happy beyond my most sanguine expectations. My happiness was, if possible, made greater when at the end of about a year after my marriage, I found a breathing likeness of my husband laid by my side. Three years after my marriage, another stranger came among us—this time a daughter.

I believe that now the circle of my enjoyment was complete. My husband, though much absent, was unremitting in his love—I had two bright, healthy children, and what more could woman ask?

Some three months after the birth of my last child, a thunderbolt fell into my Eden and destroyed its beauty forever.

My husband left one day to pilot the Lady Poole up the Ohio. The day after I was engaged in a frolic with my son, when I heard a knock at the door. I opened it, and a stranger stood there with a countenance so full of evil tidings, that a shadow fell instantly upon my heart.

"You are Mrs. F——? he enquired.

"I am," replied I.

"I have some bad news for you."

"For me! Good Heavens, what has happened? My husband, is he—" I stopped, not daring to pronounce the fearful word that forced itself upon my tongue.

"—Badly hurt," said he concluding my question. And then as if desirous to relieve himself of an imperative but unpleasant task, he proceeded.

"It was three miles above Cairo, early this morning, that it happened. He had some difficulty with his mate, a man named Jamieson, about some old grudge, and Jamieson shot him, wounding him badly."

My brain whirled as he went on, but yet there was a fearful impression that the worst was not told.

"Are you sure he is only hurt?" I found strength to ask. "Is he not—dead?"

"He is!"

I remember no more.

Then followed a dream-like succession of days and nights. I remember as one recalls realities that he has seen when under the influence of opium. A collection of sombre events —a hearse—funeral trappings—the rigid body of my husband —meaningless words of comfort—whispered directions— until finally I was left alone with my children.

I will not dwell upon the keen agony that took possession of my soul as remembrance came back, as the stunning effects of the first shock slowly departed, leaving my faculties to their full exercise. It was terrible, so much so that I wonder it did not drive me to insanity.

Scarcely a week had passed when I received a letter dated at Baton Rouge; I opened it, and found it enclosed one from Aunt Anna. In a few lines the writer informed me that she had died the day previous, and in accordance with her last request, he forwarded me the enclosed.

Another shock—but, in the condition of my mind, it did not affect me greatly. My soul was so filled with great grief, that the presence of a smaller one was scarcely felt.

I opened the letter from Aunt Anna. I have this old letter yet, and would gladly give its contents entire, were it not that I have learned to revere it with a feeling akin to worship. It was a letter in which a *mother* had poured out the pent up love of a life-time.

She revealed to me the sad secret of my birth, but told it [in] such loving words, that it took away the sting of its illegitimacy. She told too about her early love, and how, in after years, she discovered that it was her own sister, with whom she was visiting at Baton Rouge, who had intercepted her letters from Vereau, prompted to the act by jealousy. And after revealing to me all her sad history, she implored a thousand blessings on my head, and assured me that her last breath would be used in wafting my name to the throne of Eternal Goodness.

One more shock, and the storm passed. A day or two after my attorney called upon me, and gave me a statement of my affairs. My husband, with the profusion of men in his business, had never thought of the future, but had spent his entire income as it was earned. The result was, in short—there was not a dollar remaining after his affairs were settled. I was completely a beggar. Even the house I lived in must be sacrificed—there remained to me absolutely nothing.

It may be naturally imagined that this new misfortune completely prostrated me. It did not, but on the contrary it had an opposite effect.

Upon what principle this effect was produced, I know not. It may have been that of *similia similibus curantur*—or that thrusting one grief upon [a] soul permeated with sorrow, they will reciprocally lighten each other by each in its turn attracting the attention from dwelling too long upon its fellow.

Whatever the *rationale,* the results I know. By the application of a new sorrow, I grew in a day or two, less regardless of, and borne down by the others. And then, thoughts of bitter hatred began to lodge in my soul, as I reflected upon the ruin around me, and could not but revert to its cause. And who was it that had done all, or nearly all this—who had made me a widow, my children orphans, and all of us beggars? Jamieson! And as these thoughts grew more frequent, so did my hatred of him assume a more definite form, while desires for revenge began to assume shape. It was not long before such desires assumed a character as to render them mischievous, yet at the time, they were instrumental in shaping considerably the course I soon after adopted.

CHAPTER III

As MY FINANCIAL CONDITION became more desperate, my desire for revenge increased in inverse proportion. Each privation that I endured served to make Jamieson more prominent as its author, and one upon whom I was bound to visit a terrible reparation. But how was I best to accomplish this? This puzzled me for awhile—I could conceive of no means by which I could reach him. At the same time my condition as to pecuniary affairs daily grew worse. I pawned, as my necessities drove me to it, successively, articles of jewelry, furniture, dresses, etc., until finally this resource was exhausted, and I knew not what to do.

At length, after casting over in my mind everything that presented itself as a remedy, I determined upon a project, which, improbable as it may appear to my sex and to those who have followed my life thus far, I actually soon after put into execution. It was to dress myself in male attire, and seek for a living in this disguise among the avenues which are so religiously closed against my sex.

I was driven to this for many reasons. I would not, or did not dare to apply to my uncle or rather, Father, as since my marriage I had held no correspondence with him, and I presumed him to be offended at my elopement and marriage. I had learned no trade, and thus could not avail myself of any such means for a support, and besides this, I knew how great are the prejudices to be overcome by any young woman who seeks to earn an honest livelihood by her own exertions.

And more in force than all these, was the consideration that in this apparel I should be better prepared to carry out my design of some day returning upon Jamieson, with interest, the heavy misfortune he had cast upon me.

Speaking of my husband's murderer, I will say that he had been arrested, tried and convicted, but escaped under some technicality. The matter had been carried into several courts, and ended by his being set free under some informality, and at the time I was arranging my plans for assuming a masculine dress, it was rumored that he had gone to Texas. This proved however to be false, as an event which I shall shortly relate will evince.

But to return. After I had fully determined to seek a living in the guise of a man, I went to a friend of my late husband, and laid the plan before him with a view of securing his co-operation. At first he flatly refused to have anything to do with it, conceiving that such a plan would only lead to exposure and disgrace. But I persevered—showed him that it was the only resort from starvation or worse, and he finally consented, and procured for me a handsome and substantial suit of boy's clothes. This point gained, I put my children with the Sisters of Charity, and prepared to commence operations. I cut off my hair to a proper length and donning my suit, endeavored by constant practice to accustom myself to its peculiarities and to feel perfectly at home. Although not tall, my general appearance did not differ materially from that of any boy of fifteen or sixteen years—while a slight asthmatic affection which had visited me while at school, had left a slight hoarseness in my voice that assisted materially in completing my disguise. I at first ventured abroad in my new dress only in the evening, and by degrees; as I saw that I attracted no particular attention, I made short excursions by daylight, and so rapidly did I progress, that at the end of three weeks I went anywhere and everywhere without the slightest fear of suspicion or detection.

I may state here, that although reduced to almost penury and obliged at times to dispose of almost everything portable in my possession, I was at no time reduced to absolute suffering, owing to assistance received at intervals from a Masonic Chapter or Lodge, of which my husband was a member. In all, they gave me over seventy dollars, besides burying, at their own expense, my deceased husband.

My first essay at getting employment was fruitless; but after no small number of mortifying rebuffs from various parties to whom I applied for assistance, I was at last rewarded by a comparative success. In my assumed character, I made the acquaintance of some River men, and among others, that of the captain of the Alex. Scott—a steamer plying between St. Louis and New Orleans. I made known my desire of obtaining a situation, and he offered me that of cabin boy, at a salary of $35 per month.

The many rebuffs I had met with in searching for a situation though bitter at the moment, were in the end of benefit, for they removed to a large extent that timidity which accompanied my advent as a member of the stronger sex. I found myself able after a little, to address people without that tell tale blush that at first suffused my countenance, and also to receive a rude reply without that deep mortification which in the beginning assailed me with terrible force. In short, I found myself able to banish almost wholly, the woman from my countenance. I buried my sex in my heart and roughened the surface so that the grave would not be discovered—as men on the plains *cache* some treasure, and build a fire over the spot so that the charred embers may hide the secret.

And thus, when I accepted the offer of the worthy captain, I had no fear that any of the ordinary occurrences of everyday life—such as I might naturally expect to meet in the position I was about to fill—would betray my secret.

The duties of my new position, although menial in their character, were light. The captain, if he ever suspected my secret, as I have some reason for believing, respected it and never betrayed me with any degree of harshness, such as is too frequently to be found in the relations between the head and inferiors of a Mississippi steamboat. I quietly attended to my own business, and although never shunning to a marked extent the company and conversation of others, I avoided them when it could be done without exciting remark.

Once a month I visited my children; which I accomplished by going to the house of my friend of whom I obtained the suit, and changing my dress for a natural garb, in *propria personæ,* visiting the place at which they were being cared for. All mothers will appreciate the anxiety with which these monthly visits were waited for, the exuberant joy that filled my soul as I clasped the sad remembrances of a happy Past to my heart, and the keen sorrow with which I parted from them to resume my unwomanly character. For the first few months these absences were keen tortures. My children would haunt my dreams and play about me in my waking hours— the separation seemed intolerable, and for the first month an eternity.

I remained on the Alex. Scott nearly a year, and at the end of that time I obtained a situation on the Champion as second pantryman. At the end of six months I changed to the Bay State, plying between St. Louis and Memphis; and labored in the capacity of second waiter. I did not remain long on this boat, for an opportunity soon offered itself for me to procure a situation under my old captain on the Alex. Scott, and of this I gladly availed myself. I occupied a position differing only in degree from that which I had at first.

My friend the captain, died soon after my return, and not caring to remain under any other, I left the boat and determined to try my fortune on the land. With this view, I engaged a situation as brakesman, on the Illinois Central Railroad. This was in the spring of 1854, and I had been on the river nearly four years. It is needless for me to deny that during this time I heard and saw much entirely unfit for the ears or eyes of woman, yet whenever tempted to resume my sex, I was invariably met with the thought—what then? I was obliged to pay a certain amount weekly for the education and support of my children; and the chances were but few in case I resumed my other character, that I would be able to command the amount necessary for their support, without at all having reference to my own living. Besides this, as the sensitiveness which greeted my new position wore away, I began to rather like the freedom of my new character. I could go where I chose, do many things which while innocent in themselves, were debarred by propriety from association with the female sex. The change from the cumbersome, unhealthy attire of woman to the more convenient, healthful habiliments of a man, was in itself almost sufficient to compensate for its unwomanly character.

This portion of my life, notwithstanding its humble character, has not been, in all, the least pleasant portion of my somewhat eventful life. It was quiet, so far as I was concerned, and at the same time, there was a constant succession of incidents of a character sufficiently exciting to draw my thoughts from dwelling too much upon my sorrows. I might fill a dozen books of the size of this with the incidents connected with this portion of my life, but as my space is limited, I can only give in this, as in all other portions of my life, the barest outlines. I will add in respect to my River life, that during all that time my sex was never discovered, except, perhaps, in the case of the captain of the Alex. Scott; I never received an insult of any character, and when I left I had a handsome sum of money. My expenses outside of those required for the support of my children, were merely nominal, as I had no costly habits. I had regularly deposited my wages, and at the time of my leaving the River, the total with interest accumulations, was considerably over a thousand dollars.

I was some months on the Railroad, and easily adapted myself to my new position. The conductor under whom I served was a man of about thirty-five or forty years of age, named W——. For some time he paid no particular attention to me, further than is usual in the relations existing between such classes of employees on a railroad. I noticed however, that all at once he became very friendly, and when in Chicago he became generous in a certain sense, in his friendship. He invariably when we arrived there, proposed a ride in the country or upon the Lake, or a supper. During these occasions he was particularly inquisitive as to my past life, where I was born, who were my parents, what business I had followed, and a thousand other questions of a like nature.

So long had I lived in the disguise of the stronger sex, that I was far from suspecting that the motive for his curiosity had any other foundation than inquisitiveness. I therefore readily answered such questions as I could without compromising myself, and evaded such others as I could not truthfully answer without danger of exposure.

One night he proposed a champagne supper, to which, he said, he had invited a friend of his. I consented without hesitation, and soon after we proceeded to an eating house and seating ourselves in a private box, ordered supper. While it was being prepared, W—— excused himself for a little while and left, telling me to wait for him. Soon after he had left, I looked around for a newspaper, and not finding one I passed out; seeing one in a box at a little distance, I entered, and dropping the curtain, was soon absorbed in its perusal. I had been reading but a short time when my attention was attracted to the next box by a conversation which was, from its lowness, evidently intended not to be heard.

This was a sufficient inducement for one who had not yet wholly eradicated her feminine characteristics, to listen, and accordingly I laid my ear close to the partition. The very first words I heard did not diminish my curiosity in the least:

"I tell you I haven't a doubt as to his being a woman—I'll bet my life on it!"

"Well suppose he is—what're you going to do about it?"

"I'll tell you what I propose. You are a police officer and can help the matter along, and by way of compensation you'll have your share of the fun."

"Bully! Go ahead now, and let's hear how you're goin' to work it."

"Well, in the first place, you'll go into supper with me and get acquainted with him or her, and you'll be able to spot the gentleman! I next propose that we take a few bottles of champagne—result, he or she gets a little elevated—I propose a hack ride. We all get into a hack—ride out to see my aunt and cousins—nice people, my virtuous aunt and my chaste and beautiful cousins—he ! he !—glad to see so good looking a young gentleman as Charley. Well, once there, the thing is all right—if it ain't I can just introduce her to your amiable self in your true character of a police officer, and give her the choice between the jug and—and—you know!"

"Gad, you're a stunner, ain't you! You're a beauty, you are, every time!"

"Well I reckon I am—maybe I ain't!"

"I guess not, oh no, not a bit of it!" exclaimed the other in ironical admiration.

"Well, I reckon supper is about ready. We'd better go in and make you acquainted with my 'female bucaneer.'"

I quietly slipped out and took my position in the box where W—— had left me. In a few moments he returned and introduced an individual of about his own age, who seemed to be a cross between a rat terrier and a bull-dog, so exactly blended in his countenance and general appearance were the evidences of cunningness, activity and ferocious strength. W—— introduced him as his friend Mr. Rice, a gentleman engaged in the dry goods line.

"Yes, sir, dry goods—that's me!" said Mr. Rice as he scanned my countenance with a pair of fierce, blood-shot eyes that I knew would daguerreotype my appearance indelibly and faithfully upon his mind. "Yes, dry goods, crinolines, and them fixins, you know, young 'un!" concluded he, his stare changing into an intensely lecherous expression, as he concluded his remarks by a wink whose capacity wrinkled the whole side of face, including his grizzly scalp.

My feelings during the conversation which I had heard and upon being presented to Rice, were a mixture of deadly shame and fear. I managed, however, to outwardly preserve my equanimity, and answered the remarks of Rice in a jocular tone, choosing my words from the slang vocabulary in order that my conversation might accord with his, and thereby not excite their suspicions.

Supper was served, discussed, and then champagne was ordered.

"We may as well make a night of it," said W——, as at the conclusion of the first bottle he ordered a couple of fresh ones.

"There's where you hit me right where I live!" said Rice, "say that jest as often as you're a mind to, and you wont derange my affection for you not in the least! Oh, no! I should imagine not!"

Not to give rise to suspicions, I drank when they were looking, and when able to do it unperceived, I quietly deposited the contents, by installments, under the table.

"Here's to ye my dear," said Rice after the lapse of an hour or so, the liquor beginning to affect his brain—"here's to our speedy and more intimate acquaintance."

I heard W—— give him a savage kick beneath the table.

I drank the proffered toast with him, and simply thanked him for the honor expressed in his wish.

I saw W—— watching me closely, evidently with a view of observing the effect of the liquor upon me. It suddenly occurred to me that by feigning intoxication, affairs might take a different turn and allow me an opportunity to effect my escape. I therefore after a little, began gradually to increase in the number and loudness of my remarks.

"Here's at you old hoss!" hiccuped I, with a friendly pitch in the way of a nod at Rice.

"Go it, young grampus, that's me! Here's till ye, my infant progidy!" replied he, as he clinked his glass against mine. W—— exchanged a meaning look with Rice, and then proposed "a little turn around among things."

"All right my chicken!" said Rice, "count me in on that air arrangement. I know who's got a nelephant up town, tail, trunk and horns. I want to visit that animal, I do!"

A waiter was dispatched for a hack, and soon returned with the desired vehicle.

"Boys just hold on to your Dry Goods a half a second and I'll be with you!" said I, rising with apparent difficulty and staggering towards the rear entrance. I fumbled for a long time at the door as if too intoxicated to open it, and Rice who saw my efforts and my apparent drunkenness banished all suspicions, if any existed, opened the door for me, and with the remark—"You ain't much set up, oh, no! I guess not my charmer," he closed the door and I passed out. The instant I reached the back yard, which happened fortunately to adjoin an alley, I sprang over the wall, and started on a run towards our lodgings. Entering my room I put a few articles of wearing apparel in a carpet sack, and taking all my money—I had some two hundred dollars with me—I started down stairs. As I nearly reached the top I heard voices below, and had hardly time to step within a doorway leading to a side-room when Rice and W—— entered and passed on a run towards my room.

"Given us the slip nicely, by G—d!" said W—— as he passed me so closely that the skirts of his coat grazed against my person.

"Never mind. If we don't fetch her to-night I will to-morrow, if she's in Chicago, as sure as h—ll!" replied Rice.

The instant they turned into the hall leading to my room I stepped quietly down stairs and walked off, I knew and cared not whither. My course happened to lead me to the river, and I saw a steamer lying there, and from the bustle on her decks and the clankings from her engine room, I concluded that she was making preparations for a start somewhere. I entered, gave my baggage to the porter and seated myself in the cabin. When daylight dawned Chicago had disappeared and I found myself on the good steamer Star of the West, bound for Detroit.

CHAPTER IV

I REACHED DETROIT in safety, and after spending a few days in that city, I went on to Niagara Falls through Canada, stopping at all places of note or interest along the route. Having viewed to my satisfaction the various points including the magnificent beauties of the world-renowned Falls, I concluded to return west, and with this view started for St. Joseph by way of St. Louis.

I may here remark that I filled the situation of brakesman on the Illinois Central Railroad for some eight months, and had it not been for the unfortunate difficulties inaugurated by my quondam friend conductor W——, I might have staid there for twice or thrice the same period.

What became of him or his excellent confrere, Rice, I do not know. Since that time, I have not been favored with a glimpse of either—a circumstance that I consider not the least unhappy of the many which before and since have surrounded me. I am no prophet, yet am not unwilling to say that if he has not yet graced a hempen cravat, he either will at some future time, or his deserts will not be meted out to him.

During all these years that had elapsed since my husband's death, I had not been unmindful of its cause, or unthoughtful as to means whereby I could apply that punishment, which I religiously believed myself called upon to administer. I ventured upon forming a thousand different plans, a majority of which would have been wholly impracticable had I met him, while the balance were equally useless for the reason that in none of my travels did I ever meet him or learn a syllable of his whereabouts. One thing however, I finally settled upon—and that was, if I ever *did* meet him that I would shoot him precisely as I would a mad dog. In order to make this plan available, I had soon after my *debut* in the guise of a man armed myself with a revolver, in the use of which I finally reached a certain degree of expertness from frequent practice.

Upon reaching St. Louis, on my way to St. Joseph, I determined to stop at the former city a few weeks, with a view to rest myself awhile and also that I might enjoy the companionship of my children. With this view I put up at the house of the gentleman who procured me my original suit of clothes, and dressing myself in my natural garments, resumed my feminine character and occupations.

I need not speak of the unalloyed happiness which filled the cup of my existence for a short time. Each day I visited my children and spent some hours in their company, mingling in their frolics, learning their childish secrets, sympathising with their young sorrows, admiring their development, and in short doing all such things, and enjoying them, as would any mother who for nearly five years has been separated from her fatherless children with but rare interruptions. I found them all I could wish and progressing rapidly under the truly maternal care of the kind Sisters who cared for their education.

As a look back over life, I see other periods, which possibly may have been more crowded with ecstatic enjoyment but none in which there was more pure, equable, chastened happiness, than those few weeks I spent with my children. I had risen by no other aid than my own exertions from the severest poverty to comparative wealth, and from this sprang an exultation known only to those whose elevation is owing wholly to their strong arms and unyielding resolution. I was in perfect health, had the undivided love of my children, I could give them an honorable education, the future was promising, and in view of all these facts, why need I have been other than happy? I *was*—and as I daily drank in deep draughts of joy, I thanked Fate for the gift.

Although I had resumed my womanly dress and habits, I could not wholly eradicate many of the tastes which I had acquired during my life as one of the stronger sex. Accordingly, at intervals I would put on my masculine habiliments, and in this shape wander around St. Louis. Sometimes I visited the Theatre, at others I strolled on the decks of incoming or out-going steamboats, or mingled freely in gatherings of men at hotels, saloons or in short in any and all places to which my curiosity led me.

It was upon an occasion like this that I made the acquaintance of a gentleman, with a result, severe if not disastrous.

I was sitting one afternoon in the rotunda of King's Hotel, watching idly the throng that poured in and out, or was scattered in groups indulging in discussing the topics of the day. Two or three individuals were seated close by me engaged in conversation, the tenor of which I did not learn as I paid no particular attention to it. I was suddenly startled into listening by hearing one of the persons behind me say:

"I say, boys, suppose we go up to Schell's, and have a little game of 'draw.' Won't you go up Jamieson—you've had a few turns with the tiger, I reckon!"

The blood rushed through my veins as if propelled by electricity as I heard the name pronounced, of him whom I had hoped to meet for nearly five years. It was some seconds before I could command my tumultuous feelings sufficiently to look around; and at length as my heart ceased a little its fierce throbbings, I turned slowly in the direction of the group. I easily recognized Jamieson in the person of a medium sized, swarthy individual, for I had enquired concerning him, till each of his features was burned indelibly in my mind. Pulling my hat over my eyes, so as to hide somewhat the emotions which thronged my countenance, I took a long look at the man whom I so long had sought. He was not a bad looking man naturally, but his appearance was that of one who has all his life yielded to the indulgence of fierce passions. He was haggard and careworn in appearance,

I thought, which must have been the result of reflecting upon the friend he had slaughtered, and the widow and orphans he had made.

My fingers immediately sought and closed about the butt of my revolver and my thumb spasmodically forced the hammer upwards. In another instant I would have drawn it and sent a bullet into his murderous heart, which lay directly in front of me, but a thought rushed through my brain that the act would be too cowardly, while it would end the sweet anticipations of revenge which filled my soul.

The confession that I entertained such thoughts as these last ones, may cause many to esteem me less a woman than a devil, yet now I believe them in a measure excusable, as constant brooding over my sorrows had made me, I believe, a monomaniac upon this point. I had come to believe that it was a duty that I owed to my husband's ashes, to myself, to my children and to society, to revenge the wrong inflicted by Jamieson upon all of them.

As the thought occurred to me, I replaced the hammer and drew my hand from the pistol. I need not hurry—he was here, he would not, could not escape me. And so I folded my arms and gazed somewhat curiously upon him, wondering what would be his feelings did he know that the wife of his poor victim sat within two yards of him—if he knew that his deadliest foe sat close before him, and only hesitated as a matter of policy from sending him instantly into that awful Unknown, whither he had driven a few years before, a husband, father and citizen.

These thoughts did not occupy ten seconds ere he had risen to leave and I had resumed my outward composure and had risen to follow him. He passed out, and a few paces in the rear came one whose soul was raging like a tempest-tost ocean, with the emotions which his presence gave rise to—

one whose search of long years was rewarded by the finding its object.

The party passed along, reached Vine street and soon after reached Schell's establishment, entered one of the numerous rooms devoted to gambling in all its departments, and calling for cards was soon deep in the excitement of a game of Draw Poker. I followed them in, and as there were others in and about the room, my presence excited no remark. I seated myself in a position in front of Jamieson, and watched him closely as the game proceeded.

CHAPTER V

IT MIGHT PROVE interesting, were I to analyze my feelings as I sat, and watched the party before me—yet I have not the time or space. It might easily fill a volume were the record of my thoughts written—were I to speak in detail of all the bitterness which filled my soul, as recollection went back to the days which preceded the murder of my husband—of his being hurried without a moment's warning, into the dread Unknown, and at a time when life was most attractive, when he had most to live for—or the terrible height down which he precipitated me. I thought of my once happy life, up to the hour when he had crossed my path, and of my being suddenly thrown out from all this—compelled to unsex myself, to wander an outcast from the companionship and sympathy of my own sex, to labor as a menial for the pittance which stood between myself and starvation. I thought of these and wondered if he who sat before me had but known the effects of the murderous blow before he had given it, whether he would in pity have withheld it.

But I cannot dwell longer on this portion of my experience.

Suffice it, that I sat there till long after midnight, watching and waiting, and indulging in gloomy revery, which was strangely softened, so to speak, by the thought that ere long I should call him to a stern and bloody account.

It was a little after midnight when the party broke up, and Jamieson arose considerable of a winner. He asked the party to take some liquor, they all drank and went out. I followed close behind them, although at a sufficient distance not to attract attention. A few squares distant the party separated, three of them turning a corner, and the fourth, Jamieson, keeping on directly towards the River. I quickened my step until I walked by his side. It was a bright moonlight night, and as I came up he turned and looked at my countenance, but seeing no one whom he recognized he said nothing.

"I wish to speak a word with you," said I, as he concluded his scrutiny.

"With me?"

"Yes. I have followed you for that purpose from Schell's, and I may truly say, I have followed you a good deal further in order to speak with you!"

"You have, eh? Well, what can I do for you youngster?" said he, as he carelessly glanced at me, evidently supposing that I wanted some ordinary matter.

"You have done a good deal for me already, and I have come to thank you for it."

"Done a good deal for you! You're mistaken, I reckon—I don't know you!"

"Yes you do, or will in a minute. You have indeed done a good deal for me, so much so that I have for years been in search of you that I might return you the obligation!"

He gazed at me searchingly as if not hardly liking my

words, they were spoken so seriously. But seeing the countenance of an entire stranger he concluded that I was intoxicated and had mistaken him for somebody else.

"Suppose we go somewhere and take a smile?" said he, "perhaps I shall then know you as well as you know me——that is, if we can find any place open at this time of night."

"I can refresh your memory more easily than by such means."

"Can you? Go ahead then—I should be most happy to make your acquaintance!" said he, with a sort of mock politeness.

"Listen! A few years ago there lived in a city on the Mississippi a happy family, consisting of a husband, wife and two children. They were in comfortable circumstances—he able to earn a competence—kind, affable, affectionate, a loving husband and an indulgent father—the young mother trusting and happy in her maternal duties and the love of her husband."

"What's all that got to do with me?" broke in Jamieson, gazing at me with a singularly curious look. My strange language induced in him the belief that I was insane, while perhaps his conscience hinted to him that my conversation had reference to the act which had made him a murderer.

"Wait a moment and you'll see what it has to do with you. Suddenly the atmosphere of happiness which surrounded the family was overclouded. In one wretched hour the wife was made a widow, the children orphans, the husband hurried to an early grave!"

We stopped—he stood facing me and there was in his look an enquiring horror indicating that he very nearly, if not quite, appreciated the subject upon which I spoke.

"What of all that?"

"I'll tell you. The wife, hurled from happiness so high into misery so profound, swore to be avenged upon him who had drawn her into this ruin. For this she foreswore her sex, she mingled with rough men, and sank her nature in the depths to which associations with rude characters plunged her. Through all these she persistently pursued the object of her mission. Her search lasted for long weary years—she followed it unweariedly, till at length she was rewarded. This night she followed him to a gambling hell, and when he left she met him, harrowed up his guilty soul with a narration of her wrongs, and then she did as I do now"—and I drew my revolver and cocked it—"and sent his black soul to the devil who gave it!"

Jamieson sprang backwards as I pressed the trigger, and instantly drew his revolver and fired at me. His shot like mine was harmless, and quicker than thought he cocked his revolver and fired at me again—this time with better aim, for a sharp pain shot through my thigh and I felt myself wounded. I braced myself with all my resolution and almost instantly fired at him again, when with a yell of pain he dropped his left arm dangling at his side and then bounded away.

I met him some years afterwards when his departure was not so speedy or self-sustaining.

From the time that I first fired at him till he disappeared, scarcely five seconds had elapsed, yet sufficient to create intense alarm in the neighborhood, for I heard windows raised in various directions and voices and approaching footsteps. I had fallen and I dragged myself a short distance down an alley, and fortunately some obstacle hid me from the crowd which speedily gathered. Some one had seen Jamieson run around the corner, and the intelligence being communicated, the whole posse started in pursuit. I remember no more, for at this point I fainted.

When I recovered I found myself lying on a clean, comfortable bed, while there bent over me a physician and an elderly woman. I learned that I had been found early in the morning in the rear of the house in a state of insensibility, and that the owner of the place—a widow woman named Anderson, as I soon ascertained—had caused me to be brought in and placed on the bed. A physician had been summoned who had arrived just as my senses returned. The blood upon my pantaloons revealed the fact that I had been wounded. Before allowing the physician to make an examination of my wound, I requested that I might have a few moments private conversation with the benevolent looking lady who bent over me.

This was complied with, and in as brief a manner as possible, for I was suffering most intensely from the wound, I gave her the outline of my life up to the moment at which she found me. I will not dwell upon her surprise in finding that I was of her own sex, but will only add that she implicitly believed what I told her, and in a few moments had arrayed me in garments suitable to my condition.

I will add that my thigh was found to be broken, and it was nearly six months before I again returned into the joyous outer world. During my sickness I was constantly and tenderly cared for by Mrs. Anderson and at short intervals I received visits from both my children, so that upon the whole, I do not regard this as the least unpleasant portion of my life. I had the fullest sympathy of my kind entertainer—a blessing which had been denied me for many long years.

When I recovered sufficiently to be able to walk without lameness I found that a considerable hole had been made in my finances, and not wishing to encroach upon them further, I began to look around for some thing to do.

Finding myself unable to obtain anything in my own proper character, I determined to return to that in which I had succeeded best, and accordingly soon after resumed my boy's suit and was again ready to battle with life's ruder events. Just then the California fever had not fully subsided and I was determined to gratify my curiosity by a visit to the Land of Gold. A company was about forming to proceed thither, and I, upon becoming acquainted with some of the men composing the party, determined to form one of them. I invested a portion of my means in an outfit and left St. Louis to go to California by the overland route in the spring of 1855. Our party was composed of sixty men, one six mule team, fifty oxen, ten cows, fifteen saddle horses and mules. There were among us a doctor, carpenter, blacksmith, and the balance were miners and armers, exclusive of three passengers accompanied by their negro servants.

Of my parting with my children, I will say but little. That my soul was filled with poignant grief at thus leaving them to penetrate the dangers of a distant State, can be readily imagined by any one, and particularly a parent. But I believed it for the best, and steeled myself against all pleading made by my maternal nature to remain. I was tired of my life on the River, not pleased with its somewhat menial character, and fully believed that the course I had determined upon, severe as it might be to my maternal love, was the best one I could adopt. If I met with ordinary success I might be sure of a competence in a little while, and then I could retire into more private life, resume my proper dress, and thereafter in company with my children enjoy life to the full extent that circumstances would permit.

Influenced by these and similar considerations, I made up my mind finally to the step, and was soon after pursuing my way, the only woman in a party of sixty men, over the plains across which lay the distant land of gold.

CHAPTER VI

A JOURNEY by the overland route, which at the time when I first crossed the Plains was not so well known, is now almost as familiar to everybody as is the route to Washington, so much has there been written and said in relation to the matter. However as it may not prove entirely uninteresting I will give a few extracts from a journal I kept of the route.

May 31. At Fort Kearney. Many thousands of emigrants have passed here till date. The Fort is situated on an eminence on the south bank of the Platte River. River very high, two and a half miles wide and a rapid current of six or more miles an hour. It is destitute of timber along its banks, but there are here and there islands which are well timbered.

June 3. Water fine—traveled sixteen miles to-day—antelopes plenty. The plains are full of emigrants, many of whom are returning or preparing to return to the States. On every side are old plows, trunks, feather and straw beds, and a great variety of articles which have been thrown away by emigrants. Met to-day some trappers and hunters with a team laden with buffalo robes and furs, on their way to St. Joseph. Saw for the first time that curious little animal, the Prairie Dog. They live in colonies and are a little larger than a grey squirrel. No Indians to be seen, although much talked of. They do not visit much the line of emigration; although hunters report seeing them at a distance.

June 4th. In camp to-day and were passed by over one hundred emigrant teams. A Government train reported as approaching. Hear and see wolves in great quantities.

June 5th. Passed to-day a large number of emigrant teams. Overtook a merchant train from Lexington, Mo., which left there April 1st. It had twenty wagons and thirty-five to forty hundred pounds to each wagon. See no Buffalo yet, as it is too early in the season, although later, as we learn, thousands make their appearance here every year. Learn that the reason why we see no Indians, is because the Government Agents have forbidden them to visit the line of emigration. Traveling very unpleasant as clouds of dust roll up from the trains that in front and rear are slowly creeping along. On the Platte bottom we find gold wherever we dig for it, but not in quantities that would indicate profitable working. We have made eighteen miles to-day, and hear that a company from Burlington, Iowa, is just in advance.

June 6th. Pass many trains to-day. In the evening a tremendous thunder storm, accompanied by wind and rain. It is my watch and I find it a terrible time to act as sentry.

June 7th. Crossed to-day the North Fork of the Platte. The ford is wide but shallow. Twenty teams crossed at one time and there were, at least, one hundred teams in sight from either bank. Eight miles from this Ford we came across an Indian village of some two hundred lodges, and five hundred inhabitants. The chief called together some of his people and demanded of us some presents which were given. They do not understand English, but make themselves very well understood by the use of signs. There is apparently a good deal of aristocracy among them—some being handsomely dressed, others ragged and poor. Encamped within two miles of the village, and experienced during the night no interruption. Made sixteen miles to-day.

June 8th. The plains are white with the bones of Buffalos, upon the skulls of which are written the names of many passing companies.

June 9th. Remain all day at Cedar Bluffs—have the best water we have had since commencing our journey. The next day we reached Ark Hollow.

June 12th. Cloudy and cold. Hunters are out in every direction, and are so thick that they have driven the game all away from the line of emigration. Road very sandy and no timber.

June 13th. One wagon broke down and had to leave it. Are encamped to-night opposite the Court House and in sight of Chimney Rock spoken of by Fremont. Traveled 10 hours to-day. We are four miles from the Court House and about ninety miles from the Chimney Rock. To attempt a description of the former at this distance would be useless. However, from where we are encamped it has the appearance of regular architecture. It has a wing and I should suppose it to be sixty feet high, and probably it is not less than five hundred feet around its base.

June 14th. Are near Chimney Rock. It presents a very singular appearance, is probably two hundred feet high, broad at the base, and for the last one hundred feet of its height, it does not appear to be over fifteen feet thick. We are within fifteen miles of a place known as Scott's Bluffs—so called from the fact that a man named Scott perished there some time before, having been taken sick and left there by his companions.

June 15th. Crossed to-day Horr Creek, which is some 70 yards in width, shallow and muddy. Roads heavy, white sand —traveled seventeen miles.

June 16 and 17th. Very warm—passed a solitary grave. One of four brothers was to-day drowned in the Platte, near our camp. Many large trains pass us.

June 18th. Very warm and dust flying in vast clouds. Crossed the Laramie, a swift stream, three feet in depth and one hundred yards in width, and camped within two miles of Fort Laramie and Fort Platte which are directly opposite each other at the junction of the Laramie and Platte Rivers. All kinds of goods are offered for sale at Fort Laramie.

June 19th. Left Fort Laramie and proceeded to the North Fork of the Platte, eight miles from the Fort, and then left the River, and struck across a high rolling plain to the Black Hills which commence at the Laramie Peak. The plain was very sandy and dusty, without water. We made fourteen miles in nine hours. Passed a hot spring, soon after found water and camped on a rocky declivity. Plenty of eagles and no grass.

June 20th. Water plenty, roads good, weather cool and fine for traveling. Along here are distributed thousands of dollars worth of property. I saw left along the road here eight broken down wagons, and an almost infinite quantity of beans, flour, stoves, cheese, kegs of nails, spades, shovels, racks, log chains, water kegs, barrels, and in short every possible kind of property used in an emigrant's outfit, including a large amount of valuable clothing. There were also many worn out mules and horses which had been turned out to die. Found about 11 o'clock a spring of pure cold water—a luxury which can be appreciated only by those who come upon one after being hours parched with dust. Saw two graves, one that of an infant. The Government Troops are said to be close behind us. We are a little North of Laramie Peak, which seems from this distance to be at least five thousand feet high. The scenery is hilly and as far as the eye can reach is dotted with pine and cedar.

June 21th. Came again to a stream of good water, a tributary of the Platte which we have crossed already nine times. Have been six weeks on our journey. Timber along the route of a superior quality. Regretted that I had not provided myself with goggles, as the road is so constantly traveled that the dust became a most serious nuisance. One yoke of cattle became so foot sore that they were unserviceable, and we were obliged to drive them behind the wagon. Have crossed to-day the hills, known as the Black Range. Grass abundant and of an excellent quality. Wild sage grows very abundantly, so much so that in many places it crowds out everything else. It resembles the common garden sage very much in appearance, except that the leaf is narrower and smaller. We also found along here numberless insects resembling grasshoppers without wings.

June 22d. Very hot and dusty. Crossed a rapid mountain stream this forenoon. No savannahs within fifty miles. The high, rocky and clayey hills present in many instances the appearances of grotesque cities. This afternoon we entered a region volcanic in character. We pass through deep hollows surrounded on all sides by huge masses of rocks, evidently piled high in their present position during some convulsion of nature. The earth is of a color red as brick.

June 23d. Passed several pure springs and mountain streams—one of the latter is known as Beaver Creek. Road better but grass poor—drive as fast as we can with the hope of reaching again the Platte in order to obtain better food.

June 24th. Encamped on Deer Creek. A man was drowned this morning in attempting to cross the Platte on horseback. Thirty men are reported to have lost their lives there this year —it being unusually high.

June 26th. Start early and after traveling ten miles reach a Ferry kept by the Mormons. They charge us $3 per wagon for taking us over. They have a large store of goods at this place for which they charge most exorbitant prices—however they were very polite and kind to us.

June 27th. Staid at the Ferry till 5 P.M., and then crossed our wagons on the boat and swam over our teams, and then camped. Lost one team during the night and some mining tools. At this point the cactus is very plenty. It grows from two to six feet in height.

June 28th. To-day we leave the Platte and hope, for good. We pass over a barren, sterile country, destitute of water. Saw the alkali springs and streams which are fatal to cattle. Traveled all day and night so as to get good grass and water, which we reached.

June 30th. Leave early this morning and reach Sweet Water River in the evening, near Independence Rock. This is distant from the Platte forty six miles. Independence Rock is an isolated rock six hundred and fifty yards in length, forty high, and free from vegetation. Five miles from it is the Devil's Gate, at which point the Sweet Water has cut through a ridge of rocks. The gap is thirty-five yards in width and three hundred in length, and has a depth of some four hundred feet. The walls upon each side are perpendicular. From here mountains rise upon mountains till they seem to meet the sky, forming a scenery of the most majestic and beautiful character. Upon Independence Rock are cut and written the names of thousands of emigrants, and my own was added to the rest.

July 1st. Sunday.

July 2nd. Air very impure, owing to the large number of dead cattle along the route. We passed some thirty to-day. Encamped this evening near Saltpetre Lake. Here for the first time saw the sage hen—an animal somewhat resembling the prairie chicken. Game plenty seemingly not very fearful of the presence of man. This proceeds from the fact that along here emigrants are more anxious to care for their teams than to secure game. Pasture very poor—traveled sixteen miles. Every one we meet has got the blues—many have lost their all or nearly all. Some who set out with heavy trains have abandoned all except one team and two wheels of a wagon, upon which they have constructed a rude box, and in this way are getting along the best way they can. Picked up two women who had inhumanly been left to starve by some train in advance, and took them along to cook and thus work their passage through.

July 3d. Cold, with west wind which feels as if it came from snow. Scenery here magnificent beyond all conception.

July 4th. Very cold—the water in one of the vessels was found frozen an inch thick at sun rise. We can now discover snow-capped mountains in the distance. Slight fall of snow. The country is barren, sterile and timberless. We are now on the trail of the Snake Indians, but they have not as yet visited us. Are now in sight of the snow. Crossing Wind River mountains we travel seventeen miles and cross the Sweet Water four times.

July 5th. Left our camp early this morning. Saw many dead cattle along the road—their numbers would average at least twenty-five per day. Here I shot an antelope—my first essay at killing game with a rifle. I found at first the carrying of a heavy piece rather awkward, but in the present instance acquitted myself so well the company said I did well for a green boy of eighteen.

July 6th. We are in camp all day as we have found grass and water.

July 7th. Here we commenced crossing a high rolling, and in many points, rocky plain, about seventeen miles in width. Here we met three men who stated that they had got lost from their train and had been thirty six hours without food. They had killed, they said, the first day plenty of game, but it made them wretchedly sick to eat it without salt. Fed them and they left in pursuit of their train. To-day we reach snow after having been in sight of it for eight days. We passed an immense bank some ten or twelve feet in depth. We crossed the Sweet Water for the last time as we are now near its head.

CHAPTER VII

ON THE 8TH OF JULY we had preaching in one of the trains, and so rare an event excited no little curiosity. It was the first sermon I had heard since leaving civilization, and it brought back to me forcibly the events and people of my Eastern home. But enough—I will not sentimentalize over this incident, although it is ample opportunity. I will at least say that no grander tabernacle than that in which we heard the words of Divine truth that day, ever echoed the words of worshipers. It was one of nature's own rearing—its columns the eternal mountains—its dome the blue sky above.

Up to this date we had been gradually ascending the Rocky Mountains, but upon the day of which I speak we reached the dividing point, and thenceforward the streams ran westward. Two miles from the summit is the spring from which the Colorado River takes its rise. At this point we were eight hundred feet above the level of the sea, and about one thousand miles from St. Joseph.

The next day we traveled some four miles and reached the Big Sandy, and at this point we halted for two days in order to better prepare for a journey of forty miles over a desert that fronted us. Here the trains diverged—some of the party turned off to go by "Swift's cut off"—others started by way of Salt Lake City, while many determined to go by Witch Outlet, which, although the worst route in the mountains, is shorter than any of the others. We made the entire distance across the desert on the 14th, and encamped that night, very much fatigued, on the green shores of the Colorado. The next day we traveled more slowly and reached

Mosquito Creek. About this time our journey began to be pleasant again. The weather warm, yet not disagreeably so, the grass abundant and of an excellent quality, the road not greatly precipitous, the scenery enchanting. I made frequent side excursions to such points as appeared of interest, and was always rewarded by finding something new in the scenery, or some beautiful specimens of flowers or other species of vegetation. Pine and spruce were abundant, and the trees in some instances grew to a height of one hundred and fifty feet. In this manner we traveled along pleasantly enough, and on the 19th we camped on Bear River, near its junction with Green River, and in the immediate vicinity of the Fort at that point.

The next day we proceeded down Bear River and forded in the course of the day Tonnous Fork—a rapid mountain stream with high bluffs. The scenery along here was delightful, although destitute of all timber save the willow, woodbine and gooseberry. We made thirty-two miles on that day and encamped that night on Smith's Fork. The next day we were visited by two Indians direct from California, who were on their way with some dispatches to the troops in our rear. They gave us some interesting news from the land of gold, and among other things spoke of troubles existing in California on account of some order of the Government in relation to foreign miners.

On the 21st, we reached once more Bear River, and found plenty of good grass. At this place, for the first time, I saw one of those terrible monsters—a grizzly bear. It was killed by one of our party by a lucky shot which passed through its eye into the brain. It weighed some twelve hundred pounds, and had a foot whose breadth was six inches. At this place we also saw another characteristic of the country, and that was a dead Indian in the fork of a tree. His body had been wrapped in a Buffalo robe and placed there to prevent his being devoured by wolves. No sort of a house, such as can be constructed from the materials in that country, would be proof against their ravages, for they will open almost any grave with the expertness of a sexton.

On the 31st we arrived at the Big Willow, a respectable stream, and soon after crossed in quick succession the Little Willow, Willow Branch and Langley Creek. The last was named by our party in honor to the memory of one of our number who died as we reached the place. The next day at noon we reached Soda Spring, and soon after I started on a visit to some neighboring objects of interest. Among others, I examined, in a little space, no less than ten of what had probably at some time been craters. The whole country for miles around was covered with a sulphurous deposit. Near there, I counted some eight or ten boiling springs, of which some were warm, others cold, and many of them strongly impregnated with soda. We encamped that night a short distance from Soda Creek, and were honored during our stay by being visited by some squaws with their pappooses slung over their backs, on boards to keep them straight.

On the 25th, we passed an extinct volcano whose crater is some hundred feet deep and as many wide. The rocks around presented a singular appearance, they being perforated with numberless holes like a honeycomb. What produced this singular result I do not know. We found mountain sheep, as they are called, plenty hereabouts, and their chase afforded some members of our party a good deal of sport under all sorts of difficulties. In the afternoon we crossed a snow mountain, and two miles beyond camped on a fine stream called Camp Creek. The next day we ascended and descended another mountain, from thence to Indian Creek, and then a march across a country unevenly broken into hills and incipient mountains, till we reached Deep Fork, and there we camped. At this point we saw any quantity of poor-looking Indians, who came to our Camp to beg or steal something, or to trade with us some of their possessions. There were also hosts of mosquitos, who gave us quite as much annoyance as the thieving red-skins who accompanied them.

The next day another of our party died. He had been sick with consumption, and was in hopes that the trip would prove beneficial to him. He had bettered somewhat till we got among the mountains, when the air proved too chilling, and he sank rapidly. I know nothing of his history—whether he left wife, children, or other, in the distant east, to look hourly with anxious solicitude for news of the absent invalid. He yielded up his last breath amid the sublime solitudes of the mountains, and we buried him upon an eminence, and raised a rude cairn over the mound that covered him.

In the two or three days following, we crossed Panock Creek, over a high, rolling country, and then made our tedious way through a narrow gorge, which would admit but one wagon at a time, and whose sides rose perpendicularly full a thousand feet. On the 29th we passed into the territory of the Panock Indians—a tribe of hunters, who find an abundant subsistence in the myriads of mountain sheep, antelopes, prairie dogs, and other animals, with which the country abounds. We also met, the same day, a company of Indian traders, who had been away from the settlements about a year. On the 30th we crossed another mountainous range and found the weather so cold that the water froze in our vessels.

On the 31st of July, the company halted to allow the cattle to graze, and I took the opportunity to ascend a neighboring mountain to get a view of the surrounding country. I was rewarded by obtaining a glance at Salt Lake, 75 miles from where I stood. I had been told that the place was much infested with grizzly bears, and it was not without considerable trepidation that I took my ride. Fortunately, none of these monsters made their appearance and I soon after gained the camp unharmed.

August 2d, we crossed a stretch of fourteen miles, from which, by volcanic action, had been stripped every vestige of vegetation.

We got along very well for a few days after this—finding water and grass at convenient intervals—hearing news from Salt Lake City of a great dinner given to several hundred emigrants by the Mormons—and on the 13th of August we had not yet issued from the mazes of the mountains. That night our camp was fired into by a band of prowling Indians, but upon receiving a few shots from the sentries, they made off.

In the afternoon we struck the head waters of the Humboldt River—a stream of some twenty feet in width—fringed with excellent grass.

CHAPTER IX

ON THE 23D OF AUGUST we passed over a desert sixteen miles in width, and that night had some mules and cattle stolen by the Indians. The affair was done so silently, or our sentries were so sleepy, that we never missed them till morning. We were unable to obtain any trail of them, and as the number was not large it was concluded, after deliberation, not to institute a pursuit, as it was thought that the chances were too largely against our meeting with success.

The next day we only made some eight miles, as the road was heavy beyond all belief. It lay through a desert region of country which was ankle-deep in soda and alkali dust. A slight shower on the evening previous had served to render the traveling a little less intolerable, as it kept down what otherwise would have been clouds of insufferable dust. At the same time a cold west wind was blowing that rendered overcoats and gloves a very comfortable part of our attire. The 26th of August was still colder than the day previous. Ice formed in our water-vessels, and one was necessitated to the brisker kind of exercise in order to keep warm. After traveling a couple of miles we left the Humbolt, and passed through a dry cañon eight miles, when we again reached the river. At this point the weather exhibited great extremes—at night the thermometer stood at from 20 to 32°, and at noon it would range at from 70 to 80°. We met a train of twenty-seven wagons on their way from San Francisco to Salt Lake city laden heavily with goods and provisions. The escort gave us some most encouraging news relative to the gold mines, and we pushed ahead with vigor. On the 31st we remained in camp all day cutting grass in order to supply our cattle in crossing a desert of seventy-five miles just before us.

Our journey across this desert was not the most pleasant portion of our journey. Many of our cattle died on the way, and on every side we saw evidences that a similar fate had befallen not a few of those which had preceded us. In crossing we came to the Boiling Springs, of which there is nearly a hundred, one of which is almost or quite a hundred yards in diameter. The thermometer in the water, in some cases, indicated 160°. It was warm enough to make tolerable good coffee, and we were also enabled to "do up" some washing without the trouble of making a fire.

We saw many cases of destitution along the road, many of which were of the most heart-rending character. All along were the carcasses of cattle, and at intervals a rudely rounded hillock would show where slept some unfortunate whose search for wealth had ceased forever. One day I had ridden somewhat in advance of our train, when, in passing a rude tent my attention was attracted to it by a faint moaning. I rode up and dismounted when I was shocked to find within, a woman lying on some dirty blankets, and by her, two little children. All were emaciated to the last degree, and were most pitiable objects. The woman could scarcely find strength to inform me of her trouble, but she managed in the faintest of tones to tell me that several days before her husband had gone on to find feeding ground, and their team had died the day he left. He had intended to return in two or three days at farthest, and had left them provisions for only that time. He had now been gone a week and she had not tasted food in four days. As soon as our train came up we relieved them and took them in one of our wagons. Not many miles distant we came across the body of a man, who had evidently died from fatigue and inanition. The woman recognized it with a faint but agonizing shriek, for in the wasted form before her she saw her husband. My readers can but feebly imagine the terrible sorrow that seized upon her soul—a sorrow, it seems to me, heightened by every circumstance that could give it depth or strength. Thousands of miles from home—in the midst of a terrible desert —property all gone—a widow and two helpless children—the body of the husband and father lying lifeless upon the sands—what more fearful combination of circumstances could there be to give poignancy to her grief, or add horror to the event? I longed to disclose to her my sex, and minister to her in that manner in which only one woman can to another—yet I did not dare to, and I was forced to give her only that rough consolation which befitted my assumed character. Heaven preserve me from ever witnessing another scene so harrowing as that in which the poor woman recognized her dead husband.

On the 3d day of September we were still in the desert and

traveled only three miles when some of our cattle gave out. We halted at a spot where there was some poor grass, and staid there till 5 o'clock, and then started some of the men ahead to hunt for feed. They returned towards morning with the glad tidings of success. We pushed on a few miles and our guide soon brought us to a place where was both grass and water. We remained here until the 8th recruiting the cattle and then made a push of a few miles and found ourselves clear of the desert in which we had so long wandered and suffered. I have, for want of space, excluded nearly all the details of this portion of our journey, but I will say that it was fearful beyond all belief. Not only were our own sufferings intense and those of our cattle, but they were augmented by passing at short intervals emigrants whose teams had given out, and whom we were unable to relieve.

On the 9th of September we made Mud Bank, a beautiful marshy meadow of some 500 acres, abounding in the finest of grass and water.

Oct. 4, we reached the head of Feather River, and heard at this point of the death of Capt. Warren. He was chief of an exploring expedition that we met some time before on Gore Lake. At this point I met a woman entirely alone. She was mounted on a mule, had a good stock of provisions and was bound on a journey of some fifty miles to reach some friends. She had started for California by the overland route in company with her husband but he had been killed a short time before. She had taken one mule, abandoned the other, and packing as much provisions as she could conveniently, had started alone. She did not seem to think the undertaking as in any way remarkable, and I presume reached her friends in safety.

Oct. 8, we crossed two streams and reached a beautiful meadow some ten miles in length and six in width. There was plenty of excellent grass and water, and we remained here three days to recruit our teams.

I will hasten over a space of several days and say that on the 23d we camped on Deer Creek near Lawson's Ranch where we obtained the first sight of civilization that we had in four months.

On the 29th we reached the Sacramento Valley and here purchased provisions for the Mines. Flour was 50 cents a pound, Beef 25 cents, Bacon 50 cents, Pickles 25 cents each, and everything in proportion. Board the poorest and cheapest was three dollars a day.

We first made our attempts in the mines at Feather River mine. The attempt however did not prove very successful. It was in the rainy season, provisions were high and I did not find my strength sufficient for the business. Accordingly I left, and proceeding to the city of Sacramento, I endeavored to get a situation.

There were more applicants for situations than vacancies, and nothing better or more congenial to my taste offering, I accepted a place in a Saloon. The salary was $100 a month, which was somewhat of an offset against the peculiarities of the position.

At the end of six months, I became so much reconciled to the business that I went in as partner paying for my share $500 down, with a balance of $500 to be paid in three months. I remained in the Saloon eight months longer and then disposed of my share and went into the speculation of buying pack mules.

I was so successful in this that I soon after received an offer of $2,500 for my business, and disposed of it.

I next bought some mules and went to packing goods and provisions to the mountains. I was successful in this, but soon after determined to return to the States and visit my children.

I came back by way of the Isthmus and proceeded to New Orleans, and from thence to St. Louis where my children were still remaining.

I will not stop to dwell upon the joy I experienced on again meeting them after so long and perilous a journey—any parent, and especially a mother, can appreciate it without particular detail on my part. I staid with them a few months and then determined to return to see to my business in California. I determined not to go back empty handed, and accordingly I started out and bought up a drove of cattle.

Almost exactly two years from the time I had first started to California, I started again, this time at the head of a train of fifteen men, twenty mules and horses, and my cattle.

The success that had all along attended me, seemed about to desert me, upon this trip. When we reached the Alkali waters I lost 110 head of cattle, which our best efforts could not prevent from drinking of the fatal water.

My next reverse met us near the Humbolt River, when one night we were attacked by a prowling band of Snake Indians. We repulsed them after some sharp fighting in which I took part by shooting one Indian and stabbing another. We had one man killed and several wounded, besides which they shot one of our mules and run off some two or three others.

I received a severe wound in the arm, which disabled it for a time. Three of the Indians were killed, and they left and we saw no more of them.

Nothing more of special interest occurred to break the monotony of the journey over the Plains, and we in due season reached the end of our journey.

At Shasta Valley I bought a small Ranch in order to keep my stock until I could dispose of them.

After all was properly arranged I left for Sacramento to

look after my business. I found that during my absence the man had done well for me, and that my mule packing investment had proved a pecuniary success.

I assumed the charge of it for a short time, when thinking I had made money enough, I sold out at a handsome profit. I also disposed of my Stock and Ranch. I then visited a majority of the places of any note in California and finally determined to return to the States. I sent by Express about $30,000 to St. Louis, and set out to return by the overland route.

I reached home in safety, but after staying awhile in St. Louis, I grew tired of the inactivity of my life and determined to seek adventure in some new direction.

I got in with the American Fur Company and set out for another tramp to trade with the Indians on the North and South Platte Rivers.

CHAPTER X

I STAID IN THIS COUNTRY till the Pike's Peak fever broke out, when I came back to the States, and spent a few weeks with my children. I then started for Pike's Peak, going by the Santa Fe Mail route, and reached Pike's Peak in the spring of 1859. At that time it was but an incipient place, there being but one log cabin in the place. I immediately went to prospecting for gold, and continued at that for about three months and met with no success. About this time gold was discovered by Gregory in the mountains, and following in the wake of the excitement which the event produced, I went thither and located myself about forty-two miles from Denver City. Finding nothing better to do I opened a Bakery and Saloon. I met with good success, and was making money rapidly, when in the Fall I was taken sick with the mountain fever, and was most unwillingly obliged to give up my business and go back to Denver. After getting better I rented a saloon known as the "Mountain Boys Saloon," which I kept during the winter. I also took up several claims but never made anything in particular out of them. In the Spring of 1859 I grew somewhat tired of the Saloon, and went to Tarry All—a place about one hundred miles from Denver, on the Blue River. I here worked a claim with six hands, and made during that summer about two hundred dollars, clear of all expenses. I then left Tarry All and went to Cache Le Poud, a place on a River of the same name, at the mouth of the Platte. I was there some two months, but meeting with no particular success I determined to leave. I did so, and returned to Denver City and bought my old Saloon and kept it during the winter of 1859. During all this time that I had been in Pike's Peak, I was known by the *soubriquet* of "Mountain Charley"—a name that will probably not be unfamiliar to many residents in Denver City and other places in which I resided.

The second spring I was there I had a rencontre that in the end proved disastrous to at least one of the parties engaged in it, and was also instrumental in revealing what had never yet been discovered, or suspected since my adventure in Chicago—viz, the secret of my sex.

I was in the habit of making frequent excursions to various portions of the mountains—sometimes for exercise, at others for the purpose of prospecting, or to visit some sick miner. I was riding along on my mule one day, on one of these excursions and was almost three miles from Denver City, and when passing through a place where the road was narrowed walls of rock I discovered a stranger approaching, riding a mule. As we neared each other I thought his countenance was familiar, and as he got closer to me I found that I was face to face with—Jamieson. He recognized me at the same moment, and his hand went after his revolver almost that instant mine did. I was a second too quick for him, for my shot tumbled him from his mule just as his ball whistled harmlessly by my head. Although dismounted, he was not prostrate and I fired at him again and brought him to the ground. I emptied my revolver upon him as he lay, and should have done the same with its mate had not two hunters at that moment come upon the ground and prevented any further consummation of my designs. Jamieson was not dead, and the hunters constructing a sort of litter carried him to Denver.

I followed them along, assuring them that they need not concern themselves as to my appearance, for I was fully able to justify the whole transaction. Jamieson was taken to his boarding house and his wounds examined. The examination showed that three balls had entered his body, producing severe but not fatal wounds. He was cared for and soon after recovered enough to bear a journey across the Plains. He went to New Orleans but died almost immediately after his arrival with Yellow Fever.

Before his departure he revealed my sex, and told the whole story of my past life so far as he knew it, and exculpated me wholly from any blame in the attempts on his life. The story soon got out, and I found myself famous—so much so that Greeley, in his letters from Pike's Peak to the New York *Tribune,* makes some allusion to my story and personal appearance.

I continued in my male attire notwithstanding the knowledge of my sex, and kept my saloon during the winter of 1859–60. I had a bar-keeper, named H. L. Guerin, whom I married, and in the spring we sold out the saloon and went into the mountains where we opened a boarding house and commenced mining. We left in the fall with a view of returing to the States. We did so, and reached St. Joseph in safety where my husband now resides.

My children are at school in Georgia.

My father still lives on his plantation near Baton Rouge, and has written me to come home and live with him, but I shall not as I wish to devote myself to selling this work.

I conclude with a few words relative to Pike's Peak.

CHAPTER XI

THE DISCOVERY of Pike's Peak is attributed to two individuals —Dr. Russell and Mr. Gregory. I append a statement of each of the gentlemen, which has been kindly furnished me by a gentleman for sometime a resident of Pike's Peak.

Dr. Russell's Statement

As the future historian may seek for material for the archives of his country, and as already there exists some controversy in relation to the priority of the discovery of gold, the public may be prepared to decide after hearing the statements of both claimants of the discovery.

These statements are reliable, having been obtained from Dr. Russell (brother of Green), and from Mr. Gregory, and as they do not conflict in any important respect, may be considered authentic.

Dr. Russell states that a band of Cherokees left Georgia in 1849 for California, and in passing Cherry, and Ralston Creeks, discovered gold, and from them, my brother Green and myself heard of the deposit.

On the 9th of February, 1858, we left Georgia, came through Arkansas to Western Kansas, and arrived on the east bank of the Platte on the 23d of June, and to our knowledge no other white man was in the country other than ourselves. Our company consisted of Whites and Cherokees and numbered one hundred and three.

We remained in camp until the 5th of July when we separated and all left the country but 13, and after passing up the Platte four or five miles, we commenced prospecting, and found there the first gold, it prospecting from 15 to 25 cents per pan. We went thence to Dry Creek and took out $49 from 100 buckets of dirt; thence we traversed the valley of the Platte until near its head, and found gold all the way, but not in paying quantities. From thence we went to the head of Cherry Creek and Dry Creek, and found gold on both, and after some delay we crossed the Platte and took a bee line for the Medicine Bow Mountains, 200 miles distant prospecting everywhere, and found traces of gold everywhere except on Cache La Poude and Lorimier Creeks. (gold had since been found on both.—ED.)

After leaving the Mountains, we returned to Cherry Creek and parted, some returning to Georgia and the remainder went to New Mexico. We found gold almost everywhere except on the Huerfano. (gold since found there—ED.) After some delay in New Mexico we returned to the mouth of Cherry Creek and laid out Auraria, and in three weeks after, a company from Leavenworth laid out Denver.

We spent the winter in Auraria, and left for the mountains in May, and discovered Russell's Gulch 1st of June. During all this time we had no trouble with the Indians and found them entirely ignorant of any deposit of minerals, or at least, they professed to be. We went to work on our Gulch and during that season took out $60,000.

We never worked a Lode, and never more than 12 hands, never ground sluiced, and worked only the Tom. The second season here, (last summer) we took out $68,000 up to October 15th. We have gone to the bed rock as far as we have worked, and propose to ground sluice the whole of this Gulch next summer, and expect about what we have already obtained.

We first saw Gregory on the 1st of February, 1859.

Gregory's Statement

Left Leavenworth 20th of August, 1858, for Fort Larimier and reached there in November, driving a mule team at $25 per month. We found the snow five or six inches in depth and we were obliged to abandon the expedition, and after putting 350 mules in a Kenyon to winter, we were all discharged except ten men. I was discharged, and remained two months prospecting and found gold in Larimier River. I left the last of January, to prospect the three forks of this river and had with me a Mr. Jackson, and a small spanish mule.

We skirted the mountains as they were inaccessable owing to the depth of snow, and reached Arraposa, 15 miles from the present city of Denvers, and afterwards left there for head waters of the North Clear Creek.—We had then four pounds of bread, and on the day of our arrival the mule gave out, and I left Jackson with him, and alone followed down the creek to the mouth of what is now called Gregory Gulch. Snow covered the entire country, and after scraping it away and sinking a hole 2½ feet deep, I found 16 cents to the pan, and returned to Jackson that night and told him I had corrrelled the gold. I was certain the gold came from the contiguous mountains, and determined to explore the Gulch from its mouth. After three days hard labor, sleeping under a rock, I found the Gregory Lode.

Some parties came here from the valley, and from them I heard a party were on South Clear Creek, and went over and found them to get flour. The parties were the Russells, and they came over with me and we have been here ever since, they working for themselves, I for everybody but myself. I believe I am the only living being who has not been benefitted by this discovery, but feel there is a good time coming.

The time did come, for two months after Mr. Gregory left in the express for Georgia with $42,000 in his carpet bag.

A better, braver, more liberal and gentlemanly rough looking, kind hearted and true man never had a being, and the time is coming when men will show their gratitude for his many acts of kindness and attention by other than words. Had the government acted fairly, instead of the name of Colorado given the territory it should have been Territory of Gregory, as his name, perseverance and kindness, not only discovered, but his made it what it is and what it will be.

Mountain Charley

Colorado Story of Love, Lunacy and Revenge

By G. W.

[Written for the *Colorado Transcript*]

CHAPTER I

ALL THE EARLY PIONEERS of Denver, Golden, Mountain City, and the road leading through and to those localities, will readily recognize the name at the head of this tale, and as readily bring to mind the pert little woman who had chosen the cognomen and by which she was known to them while perambulating through mountain and valley, always dressed in male attire, but never making any attempt to conceal her sex. "Mountain Charley" was a character in her way, and to all save the writer of this her story has for a quarter of a century been a profound mystery, and is now told for the first time, and then only after the lapse of the time allotted to me by herself, under a solemn promise of secrecy for twenty-five years unless sooner absolved by herself in person.

My strange little heroine first made her appearance here in the summer of '59 coming in from the plains by way of St. Vrain route, mounted upon a scraggly little mule. In appearance she was merely an overgrown, pretty boy, but for a woman she was rather above the average size, fresh looking, and without the slightest indication of dissipation but always with a watchful look in her eyes, especially when approaching a strange crowd. Her age as given to me was twenty-two, and she looked no older.

The summer and fall of '59 and the winter of '60 were spent by her in frequent journeys between Denver and the mountains, often tarrying in Golden for days at a time. That her life and actions were a profound mystery to the people then sojourning here will be denied by none.

Always armed with a revolver or two in her belt and a long sheath-knife in her boot-leg she seemed perfectly able and willing to protect herself in any emergency. So long as she maintained propriety in her actions the better portion of our people showed no disposition to molest or interfere with her eccentricities, but there were certain young bloods in the camp who seemed to have an idea that it would be an easy matter to "get away" with her. They found to their chagrin that she was not "that kind of a hairpin," as she was pleased to express it.

From frequent meetings upon the road, and long rides together both in the valleys and mountains, I had become interested in her strange conduct, and on several occasions had attempted an "interview," but totally without success until circumstances threw her under my protection on an occasion when it required a few revolver shots to shield her from a crowd of drunken young fellows who had determined to make her succumb to their base designs.

It was Christmas day, I believe, 1859. "Charley" had ridden from Denver with me, and had stopped at the Johnson House for the night, where she always felt in perfect safety with Judge Johnson and his good wife. She bade me good night cheerily as she leaped from the carriage, with the remark that she would have to go out on the prairie in the morning to hunt her mule, as she was going to the mountains.

It being Christmas time the boys in town were on quite a "tear," and some of them seemed bent upon mischief, as I learned during the evening. They had become acquainted with the fact that Charley was in town, and were bound to have her out of her safe retreat.

During the evening Charley had ventured up town, injudiciously, of course, under the circumstances, but with no knowledge of the condition of the boys.

I had retired early, after a fatiguing day, and by nine o'clock I was soundly asleep, but was awakened by a couple of pistol shots. This interruption of my slumber was not enough in those rough times to cause any particular alarm, but when their reverberations was supplimented by a woman's scream I instinctively realized that poor Charley was in trouble.

Leaping from my blankets I was hurriedly dressing when another pistol shot was heard which seemed to have been fired from in front of the house, and Charley's voice rang out shrilly in defiance.

"How do you like that, you d—d drunken cowards?" was her profane salutation. "You better get back across the bridge, or you'll get another one."

Before I could reach the door Charley had thrown it open and bounced into the room, bare-headed, with a pistol in either hand.

A couple of my companions were sitting in the store, not having retired, and as Charley bounded in and realized her safety for the moment at least, she dropped into a seat. Her face was flushed and her eyes were gleaming like a tiger at bay, but neither her hands or form showed the least tremor.

"What's the row, Charley?" I asked, as I came forward to where she was sitting.

"Oh, three or four of those cowardy cusses thought they were going to get away with me, I reckon!" was her reply,

"I winged one of them, though, the sneak! and maybe he'll want to try it again in a hurry."

By this time the brawlers had arrived in front of the house, and in drunken frenzy seemed bent upon continuing their assault upon the poor girl, who seemed now to be losing her self-possession, and as their shouts were heard her face blanched and her hands, which still grasped the pistols, began to tremble.

"Sit still, Charley," I said, as I seized one of the revolvers from her now unresisting hand, "I'll attend to those fellows for you."

As I said this she looked up with a partially vacant stare, and before I could reach the door she dropped senseless upon the floor. No time was to be lost with those howlers outside, however, and as my companions raised the poor girl to attempt her resusitation I went out to see what could be done with the assailants. It proved an easier feat than I expected. One of them had become partially sobered by Charley's bullet, which had struck him in the shoulder, and with his aid I convinced them of the futility of their dastardly attempt upon the poor girl and they retired with a promise to leave her unmolested.

Returning to the house I found the boys bathing Charley's temples and chaffing her arms vigorously. After some time we succeeded in reviving her, but the fright and subsequent fainting had left her quite weak. Some simple stimulants were administered and after a lapse of half an hour or more she was quite herself again, but still weak.

Our bachelor quarters were illy provided with suitable accommodations for our involuntary guest, but it seemed out of the question to remove her in her enervated condition. By dint of doubling up our blankets we contrived, with the addition of a pile of gunny-sacks, to make her a very decent and comfortable "shakedown." After an hour or so she seemed to be sleeping quietly, and the rest of us turned in for the night.

Upon rising at an early hour next morning we were not a little astonished to find that our guest of the night before had "vamoosed the ranch," but leaving a note written upon a bit of wrapping paper explaining her absence of the following purport:

Friend G——:
I cannot wait to thank you for your unselfish kindness to me, and that of your pards. I *must* be in Gregory Gulch by 10 o'clock to-day or perhaps lose the opportunity of my strange life in these mountains. I cannot wait to catch my mule but will walk to Tucker's Gulch and get a pony from John Soot for the trip. Will you please have her stabled for me by Saturday, when I will be down, and can then, perhaps, fulfill my promise to you of giving you something of my history. Be sure you are the *only* man, woman or child west of the Missouri river that will ever have it from my lips. I am dreadfully tired, but I *must* go to Gregory this morning.
Good bye till Saturday.
                                                    Charley

The note was prettily written, in a delicate feminine hand, and bore unmistakable evidence of a superior education; its possession added not a little to my anxiety to know more of Charley's history and the reason for her strange life and conduct since she first made her appearance among us. Speculation was useless, as she had as yet dropped no word in explanation of her conduct or her aims. The reader may well surmise that the days until Saturday passed slowly and were anxious ones to me, as I could but feel that something important in Charley's life was about to transpire.

About sunset on Friday evening a boy came to the office

with a small package for me, saying he had promised to deliver it. A note from Charley accompanied it, but in a disguised hand without signature, requesting me to pay the boy a pennyweight of dust, and explaining that she had taken this method to insure its delivery, as the boy might play her false if paid in advance.

The messenger was remunerated and I lost no time in ascertaining the contents of the parcel. It had been cunningly devised for the purpose of concealing a communication which was found inside, with old papers and cloth to enlarge the bulk, and thus carry out the deception. I give the letter below, which the reader is assured was read by me with utmost interest. With my previous knowledge of Charley's erratic manoeuvres its words were sufficiently explanatory to be acted upon intelligently:

My good friend G——:

My "prospecting" is done in these mountains! I am concealed here at Guy Gulch because I do not want to go to Golden, and I have one more favor to ask of you, and it will probably be the last one, for I am going away. I want you to come to me in the morning, before sun-up, with my mule. Cinch her up good and tight when you put the saddle on, for I don't want to risk it turning with me. I'll be at the hogback north of Dick Bright's ranch waiting for you. If you can spare the time come with one of your horses and ride with me long enough for me to keep my promise to you. I *must* tell my story to some one, for it is burning my heart out. You have been my friend and must hear it, or it shall die with me. Somebody came to me last night and told me I was crazy! I dreamed that, but I am not! I would rather be *dead* than crazy! Wouldn't you? I am writing this in a hurry, and I don't see why I have to put in that sort of stuff. I forgot myself I suppose. You'll be at the hog-back in the morning I am sure. I shall be waiting for you there by daylight. I am glad I came to the mountains. I am glad I am going away from the mountains. The altitude is too great for *crazy* people! O, pshaw! Why did I not end this with my request for you to meet me? You will come, I am sure, and I hope prepared to ride with me to Lupton or beyond. I shall have much to say to you, and I beg of you to refrain from even mentioning this letter to me. There'll be no need of it, as I am a woman and must needs do most of the talking. Of course you will not mention your trip—not even to Mark Blunt. Good bye till morning.

Charley.

It may be well supposed that this curiously constructed letter added to my anxiety for the arrival of the hour that should give me the secret of this strange girl's life, and that I did not fail to make my preparations for the trip.

CHAPTER II

WITHOUT MENTIONING my intentions to my companions further than to inform them that I would be absent most of the day, I arose quietly in the early morning, after the latest revellers of the camp had retired and before the earliest risers were abroad, saddled my best pony, and with the reins of Charley's little mule fastened to my saddle-bow, started for the appointed meeting place.

Just as the first rosy tints of the morning began to glimmer faintly over Table Mountain I rode at a sharp gallop around a projecting lime-ledge that forms the southern extremity of the "hog-back." Standing there, calmly leaning against the rock was the one I sought, but before I had time to check the headlong speed of the animals she jumped out alongside the mule, threw her heavy *poncho* over her neck, seized the pommel and cantle of the saddle with either hand, and after running a few steps in this position threw herself lightly into the saddle from the ground.

There was no need for holding up now, as the girl was finally seated in the saddle. As I threw her bridle-rein from the horn of my saddle and handed it to her, she seized my hand in both hers, and with a look of most intense gratitude exclaimed "God bless you my good friend! I *knew* you would not fail me."

At my suggestion, after having arranged her reins over the mule's neck, she replaced her *poncho* over her shoulders. The air was frosty and sharp, but not bitterly cold. There are so many winter mornings here, in this incomparable climate, that are not uncomfortable to one who is taking reasonably violent exercise. This one was one of those Colorado mornings when one is enraptured with the clear, bracing atmosphere. It can no where in the world be duplicated.

Without slacking our speed we two rode on down the valley of Ralston Creek, crossing to the divide beyond as the sun came up in splendor above the rolling prairies beyond the Platte. But little had been said as yet by either of us, but what a change there was in my little companion since the day she bade me good-bye at Judge Johnson's hospitable hostelrie only a short few weeks before! Instead of a buxom, full-cheeked, healthy girl, full of life and vigor, I was riding beside a hollow-eyed, pale, cadaverous looking woman, with fully ten years, apparently, added to her age. She sat stoutly in her saddle, however, and showed no indication of fatigue as we proceeded on our journey, but showed only an anxiety in every movement to add to the distance between us and the mountains, back at which she would now and then cast a saddened, shuddering glance.

At near ten o'clock we found ourselves approaching a deserted claim cabin, and at my suggestion a halt was made for rest and to allow our animals to feed. They were picketed, while we partook of a late breakfast from my saddlebags.

My companion had expressed the wish, earnestly, that I would accompany her to Lupton, where she would stop a day or two with Judge Graham, and there decide upon her future course. I had consented, and seated here, in this lonely cabin, miles from my habitation, Mountain Charley related to me the story of her life, after exacting a solemn promise that no word of it should be given to the public until the lapse of twenty-five years, unless I should be sure of the fact that she had "passed over the range" before the limit expired. It was a strange demand, but under no other conditions would she consent to relate the circumstances of her life, which I was so anxious to become possessed of.

The fire which I had kindled in the rough fire-place of the rougher cabin seemed to cheer my companion slightly, and she commenced her story with a somewhat brighter look than she had worn since we met in the early morning. It was a thrilling, saddening narrative of young and trusting love, bareness, desertion and revenge which will interest many an old pioneer of these mountains who has long and often wished to know the secret history of the girl-mountaineer of the early days. "Now that the time has arrived," she said, her eyes gleaming with an unnatural, far-away look, and her lips trembling perceptibly, "for fulfilling my promise to you, I almost shrink from the task. You have promised, and I believe you, that whatever may happen, whether I live or die, whether I stay here in the mountains or disappear entirely from the country, you will keep my story locked in your heart for the full time of twenty-five years. You and I may both be dead long before that time rolls around. I feel it in my whole being that I shall be gone long before the allotted time; but whether I am alive or dead, unless I come to you with permission to tell it you are to keep your word. I do not doubt you, and will begin.

"My right name is Charlotte so you see I have a right to the one I have adopted, masculine though it be. They called me 'Charley' even when I was a school-girl in my old home away back in Iowa. It was a happy home, too, until my dear mother died, leaving me in the power of a harsh, overbearing step-father, who after her death seemed to lose all love for me and interest in my being only so far as I was able to advance his interests by my daily drudgery upon the old farm. I was past eighteen when mother died, but I had seen little of the world outside the village where I had attended school.

"Like all girls of my age who are passably pretty—they always told me I was pretty and I believe it—I was ambitious to marry above my station. My stern old step-father did not want me to marry at all, as it was not to his interest to lose my services, and drove from his home many a young man who showed a preference for my society. I grew tired of this, and in an evil hour ran away with a dandified looking young man who was almost a total stranger in the neighborhood. We were legally married at Des Moines when I was nineteen, over three years ago. He professed to love me, and O, my God! I loved him with all my heart of hearts, even after I found out that he was nothing but a gambler and a villain of the deepest cast. His "profession" as he called it, kept him much from me, but I clung to him like a true and loving wife.

"We remained in Des Moines for more than a year, and there my baby was laid in my arms—dead! Heavens, how I loved and mourned over my poor little dead baby, only to receive cruel chidings from my brute of a husband. I could not control my feelings; he struck me and left me there, destitute.

"They told me he had gone away with another woman, one with whom he had been associating for almost the whole time of our married life. When they told me that, all my great love for him turned to hate, even more intense than had been the love which had filled my whole being. This feeling of hatred for my husband and the low-down wench for whom he had left me, buoyed me up to strive for a livelihood and the means to follow them to secure my revenge.

"I left Des Moines for a place nearer the border, as I felt assured that they had sought a home further west. Remunerative employment at St. Joe enabled me to save some money, a good deal for me, who had never had a dollar that I could call my own, and last Spring, when the emigration commenced to move across the river bound for Pike's Peak, I had more than six hundred dollars of my earnings, all in bright gold pieces. It was like a countless treasure to me, for I felt that it would enable me to pursue and overtake those who had ruined my happiness.

"Something told me that my husband would push on to the new El Dorado with the first emigration, and my plans for his pursuit were made with as much deliberation and confidence as though I had seen him start and had followed his very steps with my eyes. It seems so strange when I think of it, but I knew it then as well as I know it now.

"For the first time in my life I put on male attire last Spring in St. Joe. It was done in sport at first, but the girls who were with me said nobody in the world would know me for a woman in that disguise. This put a new idea into my head. Why could I not carry out my purpose better so than in my real character? The time had arrived for a start on the warpath, and why not start so? The resolution was adopted at once, and in a suit of butternut clothing I went to Bill Young's corral and bought that dear little mule out there, with his complete outfit, and started across the river in April. Not even the men whom I had seen daily in St. Joe for weeks recognized me. The excitement of the start and the realization of my errand buoyed me up, and the first day I rode thirty miles to a camp of emigrants; with them I continued my journey for a day or two. Their movements were too slow for me, however, and I struck out alone again. I remember seeing your outfit on Little Blue, where you divided up with your back-sliding partners to see them return to the river with "Pike's Peak or Bust" replaced by "Busted" on their wagon-sheets. I saw you many times afterwards while we were crossing the plains, and was one of the big crowd that arrived at Cherry Creek with you when our journey was ended, but you did not know it.

"To go back to the plains again: I heard of my husband and his paramour at Kearney, and again from McDonald at Cottonwood. He had stopped there several days to practice his "profession" upon the emigrants. I heard of them again at Jack Morrow's, where he had tarried a couple of weeks. From there he must have passed directly through, as I could hear of him no more. I *knew* I would find them, and I *did!* It took me all summer, though, and until yesterday. *I found them!*"

The last words were uttered almost in a scream, as the excited, almost crazed girl leaped to her feet in frenzy, and dashed madly out into the open air. By the time I had gathered my wits a little and followed her out of the cabin she had leaped upon the back of her mule, the bridle hanging to the horn of the saddle and the lariat dragging after, she was dashing off over the prairies at a fearful pace. I proceeded more calmly to prepare my pony for mounting, hardly knowing whether to follow after her or to take the trail for home. While revolving the matter in my mind I looked out upon the prairie in the direction she had taken. She had disappeared around a jutting mesa, but in a few moments I was astonished to see her returning at a calm hand-gallop. As she rode up to me I saw that her countenance had resumed something of its calmness. Leaning over the saddle she placed both her hands upon my shoulders and fastened her gleaming eyes upon mine.

"Oh! I wish I could cry!" she gasped, and leaped to the ground.

While she was placing the bridle upon the mule and gathering up her long lariat I tried to address some soothing words to her, but she stopped me with a sudden "Hush! You know it all now, as I told you you should. I am so glad you come out with me, for if you had not I should have been plumb crazy by this time. I don't want to take you any further away, for it will take you 'till midnight to get home as it is. I don't want to stay in Pike's Peak any longer now, but I have no where else to go. You will hear from me bye and bye, if any body does."

There I parted with my strange little companion. She bade me a cheerful good bye, and rode away over the prairie towards the Platte, whose long line of cottonwoods could be plainly seen in the distance. With plenty to think of on my lonely return to Golden, I rode off towards the mountains, reaching my home as the night was well advanced.

CHAPTER III

THE CIRCUMSTANCES under which I had parted with the heroine of this somewhat strange and disconnected narrative were calculated to lead me to suppose that the next news I should receive of her would be of a more tragic character, but it did not prove so. I have but little more to write of her life for the reason that I know but little. Late in the fall of '60 I received a short note from her dated at Albuquerque, New Mexico, in which she reverted to our parting, reminding me of my promise regarding her story. She said she might go on to Old Mexico, but the whole tone of the letter was one of uncertainty.

In 1861 I saw her once in Denver, where she was engaged in dealing faro in old Dick Wooten's rooms on Ferry street. She was then elaborately dressed in the wardrobe of her sex, her short cropped brown hair concealed by a most stunning blond coifeur. Upon seeing me in the room she gave no sign of recognition that could be noticed by the players, but after another deal or two from the box she arose, turned over her chair to her "lookout" and walked out of the room. As she passed where I was standing she spoke a few low words in Spanish giving me a hint to meet her outside. I paid no attention to her of course, as I readily saw that she did not desire it known by the rough crowd in the room that I had recognized her. After a lapse of a sufficient time I passed out, and had a few moments conversation with her, learning something of her proposed movements in the future. She told me she came back "dead broke" and was trying to earn money enough to return to Iowa.

After this more than three years elapsed before I saw her again, and for the last time. The circumstances of our meeting then were so curious and unexpected that I will relate them, and then close this rather lengthy narrative.

The war had been in progress nearly all of the time since I had seen Charley last in Denver. I was serving with my regiment in Missouri, and in the fall of '64 was participating in the campaign against Gen. Price. It was on the evening of the day of the hard-fought battle of Westport. Our troops were bivouacked some miles beyond the battle field, having driven the enemy until darkness had brought to an end a hard and exciting day's work. An orderly in the Federal uniform enquired for me of one of the camp-guards, and when my position was pointed out informed me that Gen. Curtis desired me to report at headquarters at once. Of course I arose and started for the general's quarters, under the guidance of the orderly. No sooner were we out of hearing of the camp-guard than my conductor excitedly seized my hand, at the same time whispering in my astonished ear words that told me that the messenger from headquarters was none other than "Mountain Charley," in the character of a soldier. I was almost paralyzed with astonishment for a moment, but soon regained my equilibrium.

"For God's sake, Charley, what are you doing here?" said I, as soon as I could command the words.

"Oh, I'm all right," was her cheery reply; "I'm serving my country in the exalted position of orderly for the general commanding just now."

In the course of a hurried conversation as we proceeded towards the bivouac of General Curtis, Charley informed me that she was an "enlisted man" in an Iowa regiment, and had already served over two years without her sex being detected by her comrades.

After reporting to the general and receiving orders that required the return of a man with me to my camp, I said to General Curtis, "I suppose I can take this man back with me, as he knows the trail?"

"Certainly sir," was the reply; "but let there be no delay in his return."

This necessitated some lively talk between us on our way back to my camp. Charley informed me that she had made herself indispensable to the general during this campaign, and she had frequently acted as spy.

"By the way," said she. "I have been in Gen. Shelby's camp for an hour tonight, since we got through with the fight. You'll be astonished when I tell you I saw our old Golden friend George Jackson over there. He's on Joe Shelby's staff, and I'll bet you he's one of his best fighters. Of course he did not recognize me in butternut petticoats, although he bought a half dozen fresh eggs from me for his supper. He's the same old George, jolly, big hearted, and a fighter from the the word go! I'll bet you. Wouldn't he think it funny if he knew he'd been fighting *you* all day?'

This was interesting news for me, but we had no time to prolong our *tete-a-tete* without creating suspicion. The papers required by the general were produced and handed to the orderly. As she saluted in true military style and turned to depart she said to me in low tones, "if we live through tomorrow's fight I'll manage to see you again."

This was the last I have ever seen or heard of "Mountain Charley." The following days of fighting at Mine Creek, at Newtonia, the skirmish on the advance to the Arkansas, were full of excitement and peril. Whether she was killed, wounded, or taken prisoner I never knew, but I am sure if nothing of this kind had befallen her she would have kept her promise.

This ends my somewhat disjointed narrative because I know nothing more of my little heroine. I am sure it will be perused with interest by many of the pioneers who knew her. I have kept my promise to her of secrecy for twenty-five years, as that promise was given to her on one of the last days of December, in the year of our Lord 1859, and in the year of "Pike's Peak" the 1st.

MOUNTAIN CHARLEY: A SEQUEL

BY G. W.

CHAPTER I

WHEN I WROTE for publication the disconnected tale of the life of Mountain Charley, published in the issue of *The Transcript* of January 14th, I little thought it would be the means of giving me further particulars of the life of this strange but interesting character. The tale left her, it will be remembered by those who perused the narrative, as a soldier boy and participant in the celebrated "Price Raid" in Missouri, on her return from my bivouac to the headquarters of Gen. Curtis in the field, near the sanguinary battle-field of Westport.

Less than five weeks have elapsed since the appearance of this narrative and I am enabled, by mere accident, to continue it from the point in her life where all knowledge of her at that time closed. The following letter will explain how I am enabled to go on with a sequel to this, to me, interesting story:

G——, M—— COUNTY, IOWA,
FEBRUARY 8, 1885.

My old friend G. W.:

You may well realize my surprise when I yesterday was shown a copy of your paper by a friend who is a resident of a neighboring town, and whose husband has been a subscriber for a number of years. This lady was much interested in your sketch of Mountain Charley, as she said her husband well remembered her when he was a resident of Golden twenty-five years ago, and had often wondered what had become of the strange girl so well known in those days in the Rocky Mountains. Her surprise and interest was nothing, you may well imagine, to what it would have been had she known that the staid matron to whom she was showing the paper was the veritable heroine of that tale of the wild early days in your beautiful valley and mountains.

My surprise and interest were also great as was my gratification to find that you had kept your promise made to me so many years ago. And now, in part payment for the kindly manner in which you have treated my wild escapade, fully assured that my secret, so far as it relates to my present whereabouts will be safe with you, I resolved to at once write you of it.

It is more than twenty years since we parted in the darkness in your bloody camp in front of Westport, and we are both that much older. I have been married to one of God's noblemen now for more than eighteen years, and I have always tried to be a good wife to him, and you will not look upon it as egotism when I tell you I am beloved by him and my four children as few women are loved. God knows I would not for the whole world that he should know of my former life, and that is the only secret I ever had from him.

You befriended me when I was in a great strait, and I feel that it is but justice that you should have the story of my life after we were separated by the inexorable fortunes of war. I send you with this a little memorandum book which contains the diary kept by me of all the important incidents in my strange life from that hour until the day I was led to the alter by one who I have ever since tried to prove myself worthy of. Use it as you think best. I will not ask you to preserve the secret of my residence as I know in my heart you will do it. I will not insult my dear husband, the father of my loved children, by giving, even to *you,* his name, although you knew him better than you knew me in those early Colorado days.

I do not dare ask you to send *me* a copy of your paper, but I shall see it. If you use my diary to complete the story of my wild, strange masquerade as "Mountain Charley," it may prove of interest to many of the old timers—*"Barnacles"* I see you call them now, and I shall be satisfied as long as they have no means of penetrating our secret.

Good by and God bless you.

The reader can well imagine my gratification at the receipt of Charley's diary, which will aid me greatly in completing a narrative that I had before no hope of continuing.

First, for the gratification of the old-timers who feel an interest in what became of her after leaving Colorado, I will give a short sketch of her wanderings in "Pike's Peak," before her return to the states and her final enlistment in the army. This information, as well as that relating to her subsequent service is gleaned from the pages of her diary, but the particulars of adventures of many of the characters which will be woven into the sketch came to my knowledge personally or from the participants themselves.

In the spring of '62 Charley found her way south to New Mexico as far as Albuquerque, spending some time in the mountains west of Maxwell's ranch, where she engaged in prospecting on the headwaters of Ute Creek. At Fort Union she found a government train about starting for the states, with which she enlisted as a "mule-whacker," remaining with it through its whole slow journey to Leavenworth, Kansas. Here she received her pay from the government, amounting to quite a sum, as shortly after starting from Union she had been appointed assistant wagon-master in place of the man who had started in that position, he having been "reduced to the ranks" for drunkenness. At Leavenworth she was offered the position of wagon-master for the return trip by the quartermaster, but declined, as she felt that she had seen enough of the plains and mountains. Not even her most intimate acquaintances in the train suspected her sex. At the special request of the quartermaster at the post she remained there long enough to superintend the loading of the train, and then started for Iowa. The war was then in full progress, and upon her arrival near her old home her heart failed her when she contemplated resumption of her girl-life among her former friends who had known of her unfortunate marriage.

Recruiting was in full blast at Keokuk, where she arrived in September, and her mind was soon made up to enlist, which she did in the ——th Iowa Cavalry under the name of Charles Hatfield, being enabled from her general healthy and robust appearance and the anxiety to secure recruits, to pass the examining surgeon without a critical examination that would under other and less favorable circumstances have resulted in the discovery of her sex.

Shortly after her enlistment she was detailed as a clerk at headquarters, where she became a favorite with the Adjutant General and all about the office, on account of her quiet demeanor and excellent penmanship. When her regiment was ordered to the front she was left on detached services at headquarters, where she remained on duty until General Curtis took the field in Missouri, when at the special request of Major Charlot, General Curtis' Adjutant General, she was assigned to duty with him.

It is needless to follow her wanderings, which were quite uneventful until we find her with General Curtis in Missouri, in the fall of '64, in front of the advancing forces of General Price, at Independence, in the capacity of an orderly, attached to the headquarters of the commanding general.

Here she was brought into frequent contact with the officers and men of the 2nd Colorado Cavalry and the 1st Colorado Battery, many of whom she had known personally in the mountains, and was frequently compelled to use considerable strategy to prevent recognition.

Gen. Curtis' advance—the 2d Colorado, 15th and 11th Kansas and some Kansas and Missouri Militia, under General Blunt, had met Price's advance at Lexington, had met Bill Anderson's scouts in the river bottom and cut him to pieces, Anderson himself being killed in the skirmish, Gen. Blunt being driven back to the Little Blue where another stand was made. With the small force under General Curtis he only hoped to delay the enemy in his advance until Gen. Pleasanton, with his large force, could come up with General Price, who was making rapid strides towards Kansas, his objective point being Fort Leavenworth, which he hoped to capture.

General Blunt with his rough riders always had the rear of Gen. Curtis' forces as Fighting Joe Shelby's gallant Brigade did the advance of Price's army, thus throwing these two howling commands together in all of these wild dashes for supremacy. The brunt of the sanguinary fight at Little Blue was borne by these two brigades. Here Captain George Todd, of Shelby's advance, and Maj. J. Nelson Smith of the 2d Colorado, both fell in the open field, in plain sight of each other, and almost at the same moment. Blunt held the enemy at here as long as possible and then fell back to and through Independence, closely pursued by Shelby, the last tilt of the day being in the city square between Capt. Maurice Langhorn's Company of Shelby's Brigade and F Squadron of the 2nd Colorado, under command of the writer. As afterwards ascertained this little episode might be considered quite appropriate, as Independence was the home of Capt. Langhorn and most of his men, while it had been the station occupied by F Squadron during all of the previous season.

Gen. Curtis' forces fell back to the vicinity of Kansas City and Gen. Price's command advanced to Big Blue and went into camp.

During the whole of this exciting day Charley had been riding here and there over the field carrying orders and messages between headquarters and different parts of the command, several times being at the front during the many skirmishes, but had fortunately escaped through it all without a scratch. As this had been her first experience in active field work in front of the enemy both Gen. Curtis and Major Charlot bestowed great praise upon her for coolness and bravery. After the day's fighting was over the general greatly desired to ascertain something of the intentions of Price for the following day, and so expressed himself in Charley's hearing. Upon hearing this Charley conceived the idea of finding her way into Price's camp, if she could obtain permission. Gen. Curtis had established his headquarters tent in the yard of a large house in the suburbs of Kansas City for the night, and without further delay Charley started for the kitchen and obtained from one of the servants an old dress and other female fixings, supplemented by a regulation Missouri butternut sun-bonnet. In this outfit she rigged herself out in haste and made her appearance in the yard. Being unobserved she walked around to the front of the tent and rapped upon the tent-pole.

"Come in," responded Maj. Charlot, without looking up from his writing.

"Please, sir," said Charley, "my pau wants to know if you-'uns wouldn't like to buy some eggs for your supper."

Hearing a female voice the gallant major turned around to find his visitor within a foot or two of his camp-stool, and looking intently over his shoulder.

"Why no, my girl; you will have to see our mess-cook about that."

"Be you the general?" querried Charley, in a modest, interested manner.

"Oh no; I am not the general,'" responded Charlot, becoming considerably amused at his visitor's manner; "here comes General Curtis now," he continued as the general entered the tent.

"General," said he, "here is a young lady enquiring for you."

"Ah," said he, kindly, "what can we do for you, Miss?"

"Oh, nothing much," said Charley, "only I told my pau I was bound to get a good look at you'uns down here, and now I'm ready to 'lite out.'"

As she said this Charley pulled her old sun-bonnet from her head, took the position of a soldier and saluted in true soldierly style. Neither General Curtis or Major Charlot were easily surprised, but this sudden denouement knocked them clear out of time in that regard, and for a moment or two neither could do aught else but laugh.

"Well, well, I declare! Hatfield, what does this mean?" said the astonished general.

Charley explained that he wished to give them a trial to ascertain whether they would recognize her in the disguise. both protested that the deception was perfect, and then she asked permission to try and visit the camp of the enemy.

After much cautionary advice, and giving her more fully the points which he desired to gain knowledge of, General Curtis gave his consent for her to make the trial.

Charley lost no time in completing her preparations, and in a few moments passed out beyond the line of sentinels and disappeared in the timber beyond.

Meanwhile General Price's advance—Shelby's Brigade—had moved forward to the east bank of Big Blue and had bivouaced in the timber upon the bluff overlooking the ford, as the twilight was beginning to deepen into darkness.

CHAPTER II.

THE NIGHT was clear and star-lit. The pickets of both armies were keeping watch on either side of the Blue, within easy hearing of each other, and during the night many were the bantering challenges that were exchanged by the watchers.

Shortly after darkness had settled upon the tired armies Shelby's Field-Officer-of-the-Day was returning from his visit to his outposts, and as he was riding leisurely along through a heavy body of timber with his orderly he was startled by a suppressed sob that seemed to come from some one close by his side. Turning hastily in his saddle he espied a female leaning against a tree within a few feet of him. Being wide-awake to his duty he challenged her, of course, receiving in answer at first only renewed and frantic sobbing.

"What's the matter my girl?" he asked, dismounting from his horse; "how came you here at this time of night I'd like to know?"

After a little renewed crying and semblance of fright the girl told her story in broken sentences:

"Why, mister, I've been so scared all the afternoon that

I'm e'n amost crazy. My mau wanted me to go to Kansas City with some eggs. I hadn't got down to the branch here, before them Yankees began to pile down the road. When I seen 'em coming I broke for the bresh mighty quick, and I've been hid over there all the afternoon. When I seen you-'uns had druv them over the branch I was jest as 'fraid, and didn't know what to do."

"Well, sis," said the officer, good-naturedly, "you *have* had a pretty rough time of it. How far is it to your home?"

"Oh, it ain't much over a quarter from here, but I'm so 'feared to move when there are so many all through the bresh."

"Are your people Union or Confederate?" asked her companion, more for the purpose of continuing the conversation than in the expectation of gaining the information asked for.

"We all have to be Union while the Yanks are here," she replied, laughing faintly, "but now you all are here I reckon we'll have to be rebs."

The officer saw the point and laughed heartily at this sally; but time was passing and he did not wish to delay his return longer.

It is needless to inform the reader that this poor lost, frightened girl was "our Charley." The officer was Major Arthur McCoy, of Gen. Shelby's staff, who has been described to be by one of his comrades as tall, boney and slim, with brown hair, gray eyes, and for cool impudent dare-deviltry and bravery in battle, had not an equal in the whole command. Always a volunteer for any desperate scout or service, never at rest, and always doing some devilment either to the enemy or playing some practical joke on some of his own command, Shelby himself not excepted. My informant goes on to say that Major McCoy was a great friend of Frank and Jesse James, and would always have them with him in all desperate undertakings whenever he could and that was tolerably often.

Such was the man who found Charley in the timber and had taken her in, but he had treated her kindly. He told her it would be his duty to take her to Gen. Shelby's headquarters, and with his permission he would furnish her an escort to her home.

Although just what she desired Charley put in a demurrer to the arrangment on the score of timidity at the prospect of meeting so many rough men in the camp. McCoy was inexorable, however, and ordering his orderly to dismount he lifted her upon the horse, Charley still having her basket of eggs upon her arm. Remounting his horse, the orderly leading the one he had been dismounted from, this queer cavalcade moved forward in force towards Gen. Shelby's bivouac, which was reached in a few moments.

As they approached the campfire a number of officers and men were seen around it, each one with a long stick in his hand upon the end of which was a goodly sized piece of beef, held to the fire industriously, as it seemed, to enable the holders to secure their supper before retiring for the night.

As McCoy approached the circle with his charge, he shouted out gleefully, "Hey, there, boys! You'll have to lay another cover there. I've brought the general a lady visitor!"

As the new arrivals proceeded to dismount, Gen. Shelby, who was himself one of the hungry cooks around the fire, without neglecting his roast answered McCoy's salutation with, ——

"See here, Mac., what sort of devilment are you up to now? You had better cut you a chunk out of that steer over there and get about preparing your evening meal."

"That's all right," replied Mac., "but if you all have got any Lincoln shin-plaster about your clothes here's a chance to secure something for a dessert. But business first, General. Here's a girl I found out here in the timber who says she has been hiding between the two armies all the afternoon and I thought it best to bring her in to you. Speak up, Miss, and tell the General your story."

For a modest unassuming Missouri country girl this would have been an embarrassing situation, with a dozen or more pairs of eyes fastened upon her. Charley played her part well, however, and answered all questions without creating any suspicion of her true character. After hearing the tale as before told to McCoy Gen. Shelby began pumping her as to her knowledge of the Union forces in the vicinity.

"I suppose you have seen a good deal of the Yankee troops around here in the last few days," said Shelby; "do you know who any of them are?"

"Mau and Sis was to Independence Friday," responded Charley, "and they seen a power of Kansas Jay-Hawkers, and there's a whole riding regiment and a cannon company from Pike's Peak among 'em too."

"O yes," replied the general, "we found that Pike's Peak 'riding regiment' and the 'cannon company,' too, to-day, didn't we, boys? By the way, Jackson," continued Shelby, turning to an officer who was sitting by the fire making a persevering onslaught upon his rather under-done chunk of beef, "are all your Pike's Peakers, feds and rebs alike, such devil-may-care, rough-and-tumble fighters as your contingent and these cusses we have been hammering at to-day?"

The officer addressed made a laughing reply to his chief, and of course Charley's attention was directed towards him. Her astonishment may well be imagined to discover in him an old acquaintance in Golden, the speaker being none other than George A. Jackson, the old '58er, and one of the earliest prospectors of the mountains surrounding the waters of

Vasquez Fork. It required all her self-possession at this trying moment to keep from manifesting her surprise at the discovery, but she was equal to the emergency. As Gen Shelby had spoken of his "Pike's Peak Contingent" she naturally cast her eyes about to see if there were more present. Sitting upon a log near to Jackson she discovered another old acquaintance from Golden in the person of Harmon Clanton, one of the twenty-three young fellows who left Golden and its vicinity at the breaking out of the war to cast their fortunes with the confederacy. Opposite to them she discovered Carrol Wood, well known by her in Denver in those early days, and two or three more whose name she could not recall. She remembered Harmon Clanton well as a bright young fellow of 18, straight as an Indian, with dark hazel eyes, long black hair, always full of fun and life, and one of the most companionable fellows one could meet in a lifetime. He served during the war as a private in Elliott's Battalion of Shelby's command. He was offered a commission several times but declined. He was a born scout, and a soldier by nature, always having the confidence of his superiors, often being entrusted with desperate undertakings that many older and less brave men would shrink from. He is one of the seven now left alive of those 23 brave young fellows mentioned above, and is now a resident of Leadville, in this state.

A better or more genial fellow never lived than George A. Jackson, as the writer of this tribute has very good reasons for knowing. Before the internecine war separated us and cast our lots in the opposing armies we were like brothers, and after that cruel strife had been ended by the arbitration of arms we came together as brothers again and fought over in story the battles in which we had been face to face without either one of us knowing it at the time. Jackson was Lieutenant Colonel of the 1st Battalion Arizona Sharpshooters, but at the time I am writing of was on detached service upon the staff of Gen. Joe Shelby. As his name and that of Harmon Clanton are several times mentioned in Charley's diary and will figure further in this sketch, I have been thus particular in writing of them, as well as for the gratification of their early acquaintance in Golden. Jackson is now a prosperous miner, located at San Miguel, in this state, as superintendent of the well-known Boomerang Mining Company.

If my readers will pardon this digression I will return to my heroine whom I left "shaking in her boots" as it were, at the discovery of these old acquaintances in the rebel camp.

After securing from her such information as he could about the movements of the Union troops, Shelby told her to make herself at home in the camp for a while, and he would then give her an escort to her mother's house. She found it not difficult to empty her basket of eggs among the rebs about that campfire at remunerative figures, and the boys were soon very agreeably occupied in roasting the "hen-fruit" in the ashes as the most expeditious manner of preparing them for dessert.

CHAPTER III

OUR LAST CHAPTER closed with Charley in Gen. Shelby's camp on Big Blue, surrounded by a bevy of officers and men who were eating their scant supper and resting after a day of continuous skirmishing for a distance of sixteen or eighteen miles. Shelby had told her that as soon as the boys were through eating he would give her an escort to her home, and she was sitting quietly by the camp-fire, with ears and eyes wide open for any information that might be let slip.

The conversation among the officers was about the day's work that had just been completed, and of the enemy they had met and driven before them thus far. They were feeling quite jolly over their success, and great hopes were expressed for the result of the next day's fight, which they hoped would admit them into Kansas City.

"Well, to-morrow will be Sunday, boys," said Gen. Shelby, banteringly, as he fixed another chunk of beef which his "dog-robber" had brought him, upon the end of his stick: "Wonder if we'll get to go to church in Kansas City."

"I'd a heap rather look for a prayer meeting in old Independence," rejoined Capt. Langhorn, "I didn't have much time to stop there to see the folks today."

"I reckon we'd better push on to Kansas City," was Col. Jackson's rejoinder; "Clanton has got a girl up there, and he promised to take her to church in the evening. I vote to go to Kansas City."

And thus the conversation went on for some time, until General Shelby, upon consulting his watch made the remark that it was near ten o'clock and time for all honest people to be in bed. Turning to Clanton he said,——

"For fear you do not get the chance of taking your girl to prayer-meeting, suppose you see this young lady home as a substitute. Take a couple of boys with you in case of accident, and hurry back."

These words had scarcely been uttered when a horseman was heard coming up the road from the direction of Independence at a lively gait. As the rider approached the circle around the camp-fire he enquired of a sentinel for Gen. Shelby.

"Here I am, my man," responded the general; "what have you got?"

The man rode rapidly forward, saluted and handed Shelby a paper. As he hurriedly tore it open he gave the fire an impulsive kick to liven it up and bent forward upon his knees to read the message. It must have been of importance, as the moment he had devoured its contents he leaped to his feet, and without hesitation or delay began to make a new disposition of his troops, as cool to all appearances as though upon parade, but in his hurry apparently forgetting all about his visitor.

"Boys," said he, "here's h—l again! McCoy, double your pickets along the river. Be quick and *quiet!* Clanton, get twenty of your best men into the saddle quicker than lightening and await further orders. Jackson, I want you to take a message to Gen. Marmaduke; Langhorn will go with you with his company. Saddle up, Langhorn, and be quick about it." As he took from his pocket a note-book and commenced writing on his knee, he addressed his darkey who was standing close by, with "Here, Jep, bring me old Sorrel as quick as God will let you!"

By this time the jolly crowd about the fire had disappeared, leaving General Shelby alone, as even Charley had moved back into the shadow out of sight during the excitement. By the time he had finished writing his horse was led forward by his boy, and he was in the saddle in a moment and moving out towards where his wagon-train was corralled.

Charley was watching every movement intently from her hiding place, and noting a piece of paper fall to the ground as the general mounted, she waited until he had disappeared, closely followed by his servant, and then jumped forward in a somewhat unladylike manner, seized the coveted prize and as quickly disappeared again in the timber.

Being now fully convinced that the object of her dangerous expedition had been accomplished she was more than anxious to return to the Union lines. As she had heard the order to the Officer-of-the-Day to double his pickets along the river, it behooved her to get through the picket line before he should have time to obey, and all haste was necessary. Moving rapidly northward through the heavy timber she approached the river some distance down the stream. Here she became aware of her position by hearing the pawing of the horse of one of the advanced pickets on the river bank. It was too dark to see anything, but rightly supposing the men were some distance apart she moved cautiously forward until a few yards beyond where the horse was tied, slipped into the brush along the river and noiselessly dropped into the water, which was nearly up to her waist at this point. At this moment she first realized the difficulty she would have in attempting to swim the stream encumbered as she was with the skirts of her dress. She was equal to the emergency, however. Standing there a moment to be sure she had not been discovered by the sentinel on the bank above, she placed the precious paper in her mouth, gathered her cumbersome dress up around her body, threw herself upon her back in the water and commenced floating noiselessly down the stream. As she did so, by a slight movement of her feet she was enabled to gain distance slowly towards the opposite bank, which she reached nearly a half mile below the point where she had entered the stream. She was chilled almost to freezing by her long stay in the water, but was now safely outside the enemy's lines. She now moved rapidly up the bank to dry ground, caring little whether she was discovered by the men of her own command or not, she was anxious to reach the camp of Gen. Curtis with all possible speed, having gained much important news for him whether the paper she had secured was of consequence or not.

She had proceeded but a short distance before she was challenged by one of the Union pickets, who took her at once to Col. Moonlight, of the 11th Kansas Cavalry, who was bivouaced a mile or two from the river in the direction of Kansas City. Here she was compelled to explain her movements, which being satisfactory she was furnished a horse and escort to accompany her to Gen. Curtis, where she arrived safely at nearly one o'clock in the morning.

Major Charlot was still up, and upon learning from Charley the importance of her discoveries he at once decided to call the general from his repose.

Before delivering to Gen. Curtis the mysterious paper which had so fortunately fallen into her hands she hurriedly related her night's experience, not forgetting the rapid orders she had heard from Gen. Shelby to his officers, and the excitement that prevailed in the rebel camp as she left it.

The paper which she had brought proved of the utmost importance as it was undoubtedly the identical one which had caused such rapid movements upon its receipt. It read as follows:

HEADQR'S IN THE FIELD,
OCTOBER 21, 1864.

To Gen. Shelby: —

Hold the ford till daylight at all hazards. Let your transportation move out at once and follow it rapidly the moment Curtis withdraws his advance pickets. Send word to Gen. Marmaduke to move at once up the Blue with his whole force and to be at Hickman's Mills crossing by day-light. A messenger has just arrived with the information that Pleasanton is at Lexington and moving rapidly westward. Wherever you find Curtis' forces strike them! and strike them hard. Cabel and Marmaduke will be close behind you.
By Command of Maj. Gen. Price,

PARROTT,
Maj. & A. A. G.

This was important information indeed, and both the general and Maj. Charlot bestowed great praise upon Charley for his night's work. It proved to them that Price was thoroughly alarmed at his situation, and had commenced a movement of his troops southwest.

Gen. Curtis at once commenced his arrangements for the day's work before him by dispatching the proper orders to his subordinates. It was a long day of continuous fighting, with varying success on both sides, and at night the tired troops of both armies rested upon their arms.

It was during this night that Charley came to my camp with a message from Gen. Curtis, as related in the narrative to which these chapters are a sequel. This day's work has been called the first battle of Westport. The second battle of Westport was on the following day, and like the first was a sanguinary one, but productive of better results for the Union forces. The reader may well suppose that I did not fail to keep a sharp lookout for my friend, but my watchfulness was unrewarded, although a perusal of her diary shows that she was an active participant, and was in different parts of the field during the day fulfilling her duties as an orderly to the general commanding, being many times at points of danger on the field.

One little episode of her day's work will bear repeating here. After the heaviest fighting of the day was over, while conveying a message from Gen. Curtis to General Pleasanton, who had come up from the east towards our left, she was discovered by a couple of rebel cavalrymen who were hiding in a thicket of underbrush, where they had been left by their companions in their hasty retreat, and were waiting an opportunity to escape.

"Hello, yank!" was their salutation as they brought their pistols to bear upon her, "Whar are you gitten' to?"

"I ain't no Yank, you bet!" was Charley's prompt reply, "if I *have* got a Lincoln uniform. I took this off'en a dead feller back yere, and I got his nag, too. Wot all you'uns doing here?"

They explained the predicament they were in, and promising to get them out of the scrape Charley led the way towards the Blue, where he assured them they would strike Shelby's command, and all be at home again. They had proceeded but a short distance before they ran square into the ranks of a company of the 17th Illinois Cavalry, to whom she turned over her prisoners, and proceeded on in search of Gen. Pleasanton.

Returning across the field shortly in the rear of our advancing line of battle, she espied the two rebs she had captured, in charge of a corporal and another man, who were taking them to the rear.

As she rode up to the party the prisoners saluted her good-naturedly, and commenced telling the corporal in charge what a dog-goned liar that cuss was. Charley had a good laugh at them, and as she started to ride off said, "oh well, I guess that is all right, boys. We'll treat you well. By the way, corporal," she continued, addressing the man in charge, "you wan't to tell the provost marshall that I captured those rebs for you."

"I'll do that, sure," was the response: "What's your name and regiment?"

"My name is Charley Hatfield, orderly at Gen Curtis' headquarters."

"There appears to be a good many Charleys around here, somehow, ain't there, pard?" said the corporal, turning to his companion.

"Well I reckon," responded the man; "there's three of us any how."

This little by-play interested "our Charley" a little, and she asked ther names and regiment.

To this the corporal answered "My name is Charley Johnson,* and my bunkey here is named Charley Billington, of L Squadron, 17th Illinois Cavalry."

The whole party proceeded to headquarters together, chatting merrily while bullets were whistling and shells screaming over and about their heads.

CHAPTER IV.

THE CELEBRATED RETREAT of Gen. Price and his now worn out and broken army down the borders of Missouri and Kansas has been written of many times, and I do not propose to enter into the particulars of it only so far as the actors of my story are concerned. The pursuit was steady and persistent, in which the Brigade commanded by Col. Jim Ford, of the 2d Colorado Cavalry, was nearly always in the lead. In this brigade were the 2nd Colorado Cavalry under the immediate command of Lieut. Col. Theo. H. Dodd, and McClain's 1st Colorado Battery. Holding the rear of Price's army was nearly always Joe Shelby's fighting brigade, commanded by Shelby in person. The hard knocks these two dashing brigades gave each other all the way from Little Blue to Newtonia will never be forgotten by the participants, each of whom, whenever they have met since the war have been free to accord to the other the best of fighting qualities.

Following the days fighting at Westport spoken of in the last chapter the pursuit was continued all of the long night. I have a letter from Col. Jackson which gives some interesting details of the retreat of the rebel forces at this juncture

* I have been a good deal interested since ascertaining that this is our friend Charley Johnson, now foreman of Wells' paper mill in this city, and a jolly good fellow on general principles. He will be as much astonished at the revelation as I was myself, doubtless, and would have been still more so had he known that his pleasant battle-field acquaintance was a girl.

which will be interesting to the readers who participated in the pursuit. He says, in his quaint, good-natured way, "I can tell you, George, you made us *tired*. We traveled and skirmished with your advance all night, part of the night through the prairie, and it on fire. I was in the rear throughout the night, and have good reasons for remembering those white-horse squadrons of your regiment. The next day at ten o'clock we camped long enough to get a bite to eat, and then off again on the retreat. This day Shelby in the advance instead of the rear as the night before, Gen. Marmaduke in the centre and Generals Cabel and Fagan in the rear. About 2 o'clock in the afternoon we struck by Gen. Pleasanton's command from the right flank, who cut our column in two and doubled the rear end back, capturing Generals Marmaduke and Cabel with about seven hundred of their soldiers, cannons, supplies, etc. We then formed on the opposite bank of the creek (Shelby's command) and had a spirited little fight at that point. Then moved about two miles out on the prairie and formed our whole force in line of battle, and there is where your forces made their prairie charge, led by Gen. Blunt. We held the ground and they fell back for reinforcements which were close at hand. As soon as you fell back we moved down the road and kept up a brisk retreat until nearly daylight, when we went into camp, with our rear (Shelby) skirmishing with your advance; got something to eat, burnt our wagons and lit out again. We saw no more of your command until we struck Newtonia, at which place you struck us while at dinner in the edge of the woods. Shelby made his command tie their horses in the timber and moved out on the prairie on foot, and it was his men that your white-horse company charged on our right wing, and your left. I guess you remember that charge, as nearly all the white horses were either killed or wounded. I was at the time of the charge on our extreme right, and recognized O. D. Holliday—a cousin of mine—(Corporal Holliday of F Squadron 2nd Colorado Cavalry)—when his horse fell. He got away on foot. Your forces fell back on the hill just before sundown, and as our remaining wagons had got a good start, we pulled out down the road at a lively rate keeping it up until nearly daylight, when we went into camp and finished the dinner we had left so unceremoniously the day before. We then moved to Cane Hill, went into camp and rested two days."

During all these bloody days I saw nothing of Mountain Charley and began to conjecture that she had been either killed or captured. Just before reaching Newtonia I saw Major Charlot and learned from him that his headquarters morn-report of the day before showed Hatfield as "missing" and from that time until the receipt of the letter which introduced this sequel no intimation that she was living or dead ever came to me. Her diary enables me to supply the connecting links, and to follow her movements to the end of the campaign and beyond.

In that grand prairie charge spoken of by Colonel Jackson in the letter quoted from above, Charley was a participant. She brought the message to Gen. Blunt from Gen. Curtis to make the advance upon the enemy's line of battle, and as the forward movement was commenced at once she asked and obtained permission of Gen. Blunt to remain with him until the dash had been made. That mad charge left many a poor fellow upon the bloody field, some of them dead and many more wounded and helpless. Among the latter was poor Charley, with a gun-shot wound in the leg and a sabre-cut in the shoulder. Ten minutes after our forces fell back she was found by some of Shelby's men upon the ground by the side of her dead horse, weak and helpless from loss of blood. The boys picked her up tenderly, and conveyed her to an ambulance, she being selected from among a score or more of wounded men who had fallen in the charge; all the rest were left upon the field to be cared for by their own command. Somehow there seemed to be something about her appearance that worked upon the sympathies of these rough fellows, and they could not bear to leave her there to die, as she undoubtedly would before our forces could have reached the field on their advance again. Shortly after her captors had reached the ambulance with their prisoner the rebels were in full retreat again. The ambulance was full of wounded men, but the surgeon in charge whose sympathies had also been wrought upon by her pitiable plight decided to make room for her.

NOTE—We expected to complete this narrative in this issue, but for want of space are compelled to reserve the final chapters until next week.—ED.

Scarcely had Charley been made comfortable in the ambulance by the kind-hearted surgeon when the Union forces made another forward movement and the rebel line fell rapidly back. The hospital train pulled out to the rear on a gallop to secure a safe distance from the shot and shell that were again being poured into the enemy by Gen. Blunt. As has been stated, Charley was very weak from loss of blood and the pain of her wounds, and the train had proceeded but a short distance until she fainted. The surgeon in charge of the wounded was Dr. Jesse Terry, Headquarters surgeon of Shelby's Brigade, and as Charley found out before the day was over was not only highly accomplished in his profession but a perfect gentleman in his treatment of her.

Riding up to the ambulance as it was rapidly moving to

the rear Dr. Terry discovered that his little Yankee patient had swooned. In addition to this discovery he found that the two wounded men with her had both died from their wounds since starting on the retreat. He acted promptly and judiciously in this emergency. Leaping from his horse and handing the reins to an orderly, he climbed into the ambulance. He then gave orders to the driver to increase his speed as much as possible, and to drive up alongside of one of the baggage wagons, which was accomplished in a few moments. He than had the bodies of the two dead men transferred to the wagon, leaving Charley alone in the other vehicle. She had not yet recovered from her faint, and the doctor administered some stimulants which partially revived her. Noticing that her wounds were still bleeding profusely he resolved upon an attempt at dressing them. By this time she had again fainted and Dr. Terry proceeded to remove her jacket as tenderly as possible to inspect the wound upon her shoulder. Unbuttoning her shirt at the throat and turning her partially to enable him to cut the garment at the back he laid it back gently from the shoulder and breast. The good surgeon's surprise may be better imagined than described to discover that his patient was a woman!

The wound in her shoulder was a ghastly one, but not dangerous, and the doctor dressed it as gently as the circumstances would admit, the vehicle being upon the full jump all the time. He was too much of a gentleman to give the slightest hint of his discovery to the driver, having replaced her clothing over her breast instantly. The injury in her leg proved to be a flesh wound above the knee, the ball having passed around the bone and lodged in the fleshy part of the leg underneath. He could of course make no attempt at removing the ball then, but he tenderly made applications to stop the bleeding, and then gave her more stimulants to give her strength until camp could be reached.

In a moment or two Charley revived again, and appeared so much better that Dr. Terry resolved to leave her for other duties, although as may well be imagined, his interest in her had greatly increased. Even to her he did not make known his discovery, but cautioning the driver to avoid rough places in the road as much as possible, he mounted his horse and moved down the column towards the rear, and was soon engaged in caring for others who were being constantly wounded by the enemy's firing.

As related in Col. Jackson's letter the retreat was kept up briskly until daylight the next morning, when the tired army went into camp for a short time. As soon as his onerous duties would admit of a spare moment Dr. Terry went in search of his Yankee patient, in whom, it may well be supposed, he felt a lively interest.

A temporary shelter had been improvised for the wounded, who were being well cared for by Dr. Dobbins, one of the regimental surgeons. As Dr. Terry approached this rough field hospital, Dr. Dobbins hailed him, and informed him that there was a wounded prisoner there who wished to see him.

After her wounds had been dressed Charley had gained strength rapidly, and when the retreating column halted she was feeling greatly revived, but still very weak and tired from the long, rough ride. Finding that her wounds had been dressed she realized the almost certainty that her secret had been discovered, and her first thought was to ascertain the name of the surgeon who had attended her. This she succeeded in doing from the driver of the ambulance.

As the doctor approached where she was laying upon the

ground she recognized his kindly face as she had seen it as he aided in making room for her among the wounded men when brought in from the field.

"Well, my man," said he as he raised her arm to feel her pulse, "you have had a pretty rough time of it."

"Yes, I have that," replied Charley faintly, "but thanks to you I expect I will pull through." As she said this she drew the doctor towards her, and as he dropped upon his knees by her side she whispered excitedly "Dr. Terry, have you a wife or mother?"

"Yes, indeed I have both, thank God," he answered in a whisper, "and your secret is safe with me until you are able to tell me your story. There is not time now and this is no place to hear it." Then in a louder voice, intended for the ears of those around them he continued, "I reckon you will get along all right, and if your fellows don't recapture you we'll take good care of you until you can be exchanged."

The surgeons found enough to do during the short halt of the defeated army, but Dr. Terry found time to re-dress Charley's wounds, and giving her a portion of his own scant rations he gave her in charge of one of his hospital stewards to be made as comfortable as possible on the further retreat to Newtonia.

The people of the town having fled upon the approach of the two armies, a number of the houses were taken possession of by the Confederate surgeons for hospital purposes, by order of Gen. Price, and the large numbers of wounded were disposed of and made as comfortable as circumstances would admit.

The reader may be sure that Dr. Terry had selected comfortable quarters for his wounded prisoner, and had made her as comfortable as his limited means would allow, having removed the ball from her leg by a skillful operation shortly after arriving at Newtonia, and she was now comparatively easy, although unable to move without the greatest pain.

CHAPTER V.

SUCH WAS THE SITUATION when the advancing Federals, under the indomitable Gen. Blunt, again struck the demoralized and worn-out forces of Gen. Shelby at the edge of the little town of Newtonia, where, on that afternoon, one of the hottest battles of the campaign occurred, mainly between the brigades of Gen. Blunt and Gen. Shelby. Here these two iron commands clashed together hour after hour, now the Federals encouraged by a giving way in the ranks of the enemy only to have their shouts of victory repeated by the rebels as a counter-charge was made.

Thus this most sanguinary conflict was kept up until darkness fell upon the valley and the brave brigade of Gen. Joe Shelby was compelled to withdraw from the field by sheer exhaustion.

Many scores of dead and wounded of both sides were added to the already long lists by this battle, and as Shelby's object in making his stand here had been accomplished— to allow his wagon train to gain a good start to the rear, he moved with his whole force down the road towards Cane Hill as rapidly as the exhausted state of his command would permit.

Under a flag of truce an arrangement was entered into whereby Gen. Shelby was allowed to leave a party behind to gather his wounded and to bury his dead, and also a surgeon to attend to the wounded.

At his particular request Dr. Terry was selected for his important duty, and until far into the night the details from the two armies worked together searching over the field for the wounded and dead. Many of both armies were found and tenderly cared for alike, not the slightest partiality being shown by either side.

Dr. George S. Akin, of the 2nd Colorado, was in charge of the Federal details, and to him Dr. Terry reported that his hospital stores, which had been meagre at best, were entirely exhausted. Col. Ford at once ordered Dr. Akin to supply him liberally, and the work of attending to the wounded went on as though the unfortunate fellows had all belonged to one command, the several surgeons of Blunt's brigade and Dr. Terry working together like brothers in the same good cause, while the burying parties of the two commands were performing the last sad rites for their dead comrades in the same friendly spirit.

Late at night, while going the rounds among the wounded together, Dr. Akin and Dr. Terry came to the house in which Charley had been billeted. Before entering Dr. Terry informed his companion that he had a wounded prisoner there in whom he felt a great interest, as he was a mere lad, and had suffered severely from the long rough ride since the fight on the prairie two days since. These two gentlemen had formed a strong professional friendship during their sad night's work together, and Dr. Terry was debating in his mind whether or not to divulge to his companion his secret. When they entered the room together Charley was sleeping upon a lounge, while two or three others were disposed about the room. The two surgeons passed from one to the other, now a Federal and then a Confederate, giving to each kindly words of encouragement, and such medical treatment as was required.

Upon a mattress on the floor near the lounge upon which Charley was laying was a young fellow suffering severely from a gun-shot wound in the thigh. His long black hair was matted with blood, his face almost as pale as death from loss of blood and the pain of his wound, but his eyes were bright and possessed of a firmness one would scarcely expect under such circumstances. Dr. Terry recognized him at once as one of Shelby's men well known to him, and as he approached to his side he said kindly,——

"Well, Harman, my boy, they got you too, did they?"

"It looks mightily like it, Dock," was his faint but cheerful reply; "those white-horse Pike's Peakers fetched me down in that last crazy charge of theirs on our right."

Turning to Dr. Akin, Terry said to him, "Doctor, this is one of the wildest, bravest boys in Shelby's whole command. He is from Colorado, too, and should I be compelled to leave him with you I am sure you will look well to him and his wounds."

"You may be sure of that, doctor," replied Akin, as he stooped down and placed his hand tenderly upon his forehead, at the same time brushing his clotted hair back from his face. As he did so a smile of recognition illumined the countenance of the wounded man, and at the same time Doctor Akin grasped his hand and exclaimed. "Well, I'll be——! Why, if this isn't Harman Clanton! Clanton, you little cuss, when I saw you in Golden last, I did not expect to next see you in this fix!"

The recognition was mutual, the two having known each other well in Colorado before the breaking out of the war. Dr. Terry was greatly pleased at this, as he was now fully assured his young friend would have the best of treatment if he was compelled to desert him.

Meanwhile Charley had been awakened by the groaning of some of the wounded men in the room, and had heard the conversation just related, which the reader may well assume was an interesting one to her.

As the two surgeons again approached her, she too recognized Dr. Akin as an old Golden friend, but of course gave no sign. Dr. Terry came forward and kindly took her hand, saying "Doctor, this is the young prisoner I was speaking of. How do you feel now, my boy?" said he; "has your sleep rested you any?"

"O, yes sir; I feel quite revived, but I am dreadfully weak. If it is possible to give me a little coffee soon I believe I will be all right. I have not had a mouthfull except the bite you so kindly gave me yesterday morning, for three days."

An attendant was at once dispatched for the coveted dish, and such suitable food as could be obtained.

"My lad," said Dr. Akin, as he came forward, tenderly taking her hand, "What command do you belong to?"

"The ——th Iowa, on detached service at Gen. Curtis' headquarters, sir," was the reply, "but I suppose I am this good surgeon's prisoner now," and she cast a grateful, almost loving glance at that gentleman.

These unusual actions seemed to work upon the feelings of Dr. Akin, also, and he asked for more particulars regarding the manner of her capture, wounds, etc. The information was given him briefly by Dr. Terry, without intimating any thing about his discovery, at the same time hoping that his professional brother would make the discovery for himself, believing it would be better for the patient should she be left in his charge; hence it was gratifying to him to see Dr. A. kneel down by the cot and place his hand upon her heart. As he arose to his feet a hasty professional glance told him that his companion had discovered the secret that he would have died before revealing to any person other than one of his own profession. The two now moved towards the door, and as they did so Dr. Akin turned to Charley and said, ——

"You must be careful, my lad, when the boys bring your

rations. You have much fever now, and too much will injure you more than you think."

"All right, doctor," was the cheerful reply; "I'll be careful. But can I divide them with this chap on the floor here? He looks as though a little coffee would not hurt him."

"Oh, I reckon so," answered Dr. Terry; "He's a pretty tough cuss any how. Clanton, if you find that young Yank there is liable to gorge himself you may worry down the surplus."

Clanton laughed at this sally, saying he supposed they were both about in the same fix in regard to helping themselves.

The cheerful mood of the two surgeons seemed to do these young patients a world of good, both of them appearing to be greatly revived after the gentlemen had left the room. The detail soon returned with the coffee and some rice and milk which had been prepared for the wounded soldiers who were able to partake of it. This they enjoyed greatly, and as they lay there, propped up so as to be able to manipulate their rations, they chatted merrily over the rough times they had been going through during the last few days. Charley was careful not to allude to the discovery he had made of Clanton's identity, whose position upon the floor was such that he could not get a good look into her face.

Thus the night wore on. The wounded of both armies had been gathered and well cared for; the dead had been buried while the tired officers and men still for duty were getting a much needed sleep preparatory to an early advance in the morning which all expected would be made after the retreating foe.

It was four o'clock when reveille was sounded from Gen. Blunt's headquarters, and by five the command was in column ready for a start. As the order was about to be given a messenger arrived with a dispatch from Department Headquarters at St. Louis to discontinue the pursuit of Price's army, and for the troops to return without delay to their respective stations. This was a most surprising and discouraging turn of affairs, as Gen. Blunt and every man in the command was sure that another day such as the last one had been would force Gen. Price to surrender his whole command.

Orders are orders, however, in the army, and there was no alternative. Gen. Blunt's disappointment was shared by all, from the highest to the lowest in rank, but the column was turned northward at once and marched to the northern edge of the little town, where the troops were again put into camp for a further rest for a few hours before starting on the day's march.

Shortly after sun rise a flag of truce arrived from Gen. Price with a proposition for an exchange of wounded prisoners. Col. George A. Jackson, of Gen. Shelby's staff, was the bearer of the flag, and an exchange was effected without difficulty. He was accompanied by Capt. Langhorn and his company as escort, with several wagons in which to convey such of their wounded as were able to be moved to Gen. Price's camp.

The cartel provided that such of the wounded of both armies as were found unable to be moved should be left at Newtonia in charge of a surgeon from each command. This business occupied several hours, so that it was nearly noon before General Blunt gave the order for "Boots and Saddles" to be sounded.

The command moved out, and at the same time Col. Jackson, with his escort, started on his return to his command, each taking along such of their wounded as could be moved comfortably, the others being left in the town in charge of Dr. Akin of our forces, and Dr. Terry of the Confederate command.

Gen. Blunt moved his column back to Neasho, a good day's march, and went into camp for the night. Here peremptory orders were received from General Grant, Commander in chief, countermanding the orders which had been received from St. Louis, and to pursue General Price vigorously to the Arkansas if necessary. The following morning Gen. Blunt turned his columns southward again, but two days had been placed between the pursuers and pursued, leaving very little hope of overtaking them. Gen. Grant's order was obeyed to the letter, however, and we arrived at the Arkansas in time to see the last of the fleeing force disappear in the timber on the opposite side, and to fire a farewell salute from McLain's and Dodge's batteries into his rear.

CHAPTER VI

THE RETURN of Gen. Blunt's command to Kansas was slow and uneventful. Before his column reached Newtonia on its return Dr. Akin had found all of his wounded able to be removed, and had started with them for Fort Leavenworth, where he arrived a few days in advance of Gen. Blunt's command.

On their arrival there Charley was able to report for duty, although still considerably debilitated. A surprise awaited her here, as unexpected as it was gratifying. On the night of her dangerous expedition as a spy to the camp of Gen. Shelby on the Blue, Gen. Curtis had been so much gratified at her success and the bravery displayed in the execution of her perilous trust that he had written to the governor of Iowa recommending her promotion. The result was as gratifying to the general and his adjutant-general—Maj. Charlot, as it was to the beneficiary herself. Upon his return to Fort Leavenworth from the pursuit of Gen. Price, Gen. Curtis found a reply to his letter to the governor enclosing a commission as, 1st Lieutenant Charles Hatfield, and an assignment to duty as aid-de-camp upon his staff.

Charley accepted her new honors modestly, and with many expressions of thanks to the general for his confidence in her patriotism and worth to the service.

Upon reporting to Maj. Charlot for duty in her new position on the following morning, Lieut. Hatfield was again greatly surprised and gratified by being presented by that officer with an elegant officer's sword and equipments complete, together with an order for a full uniform suitable for her new rank, a gift from the general and the gentlemen of his staff.

Thus it will be seen that our brave young heroine entered upon her new duties under auspices the most flattering and pleasing. In this capacity she served as faithfully as she had served for three years almost, as a private, doing duty at Leavenworth and upon the plains until the close of the war in the following June. She then returned to Iowa with Gen. Curtis and staff and was mustered out at Des Moines.

Upon her earnest solicitation nothing more will be given of the life of this strange character after her return to civil life. The reader already knows, from the letter published at the commencement of this sequel, that she is happily married, and with a tenderly loving husband and a family of loving children around her, is passing her declining years in a sphere suited to her sex, loved and respected by all who know her.

In the words of Rip Van Winkle, "May she live long and prosper."